A Inappropriate Message

A True Story

Charles King

First published 2018

ISBN 978-0-244-41247-0

Copyright © Charles King 2018

For Lisa,
without whom I would be broken

PROLOGUE

THE MESSAGE

"Will you be home for dinner? I'm making midlife crisis."
"Oh, I guess I'll have a slice, if you're making it already."
Maggie Stiefvater, The Dream Thieves

It was December 2013 and I hadn't seen Sofia Messina for 4 months, but she had recently made contact with me indirectly. I was coming to the end of an awful year full of personal, professional and family difficulties. Amongst these was a strange relationship I had developed with a young Sicilian woman. 'She's driving me crazy this girl', I thought to myself, 'let's find out what she really wants... let's bring this thing to a head.' I was feeling reckless, frustrated and in turmoil at how my life, whilst superficially normal, had become in my mind complex and unsatisfactory. I knew that the source of this was the romantic feelings I had developed towards Sofia, or was it? Was there a deeper spiritual malaise going on? Was my instability connected to previous tragedy and guilt? Had a recent family bereavement taken its toll on me? I had plenty of questions in my mind, but very few answers. I had come to the conclusion that if I were to move on in life I needed Sofia either more closely connected to me, supporting me, or out of my life altogether. If this relationship was going to go anywhere, I needed to find out whether I could trust her, for my instincts were telling me I could not. I felt an urgent need to do something that would let me know whether we had a future together. 'I need to tell her I love her,' I thought to myself. 'Then we'll find out what she really wants.'

Of course, all this thinking was absurd and ridiculous; the product of a self-obsessed man in the throes of a mid-life crisis. A man whose grip on reality was severely compromised. A man who had lost the plot. I had stopped thinking and caring for other people and turned inward on myself. I was heading for disaster and staring into the abyss.

My first step to disaster was to send Sofia an affectionate message which I did late on a Friday night a few days before Christmas. I had imbibed an excessive amount of whisky:

"My dear Sofia, it was good to hear your news. You're a very special person and I can't tell you how much I've missed you. But I guess it's my own fault for cutting off contact from you. I'm doing well and looking forward to the staff pantomime in January. I've been cast as a pirate and am wondering whether I should do a West Country or London accent...."

This was the first message I had sent to Sofia for three months. I doubted that she would reply and indeed, part of me hoped that she would not, but the following afternoon a message was forthcoming from her:

"Your words are lovely but I don't understand why you blocked me?? I never expected that from someone like you ☹"

Her double question marks and confused face cried out to me. She's asking for answers, she's asking for the truth, so let's go for it – ' let's tell her how I really feel', screamed my ego urged on by my id. So, I dived into oblivion with the message that would seal my fate; the message that started a series of events which changed my life irrevocably. Impulsively, I found myself writing the following:

"I know, it was cruel, but I was losing control of my emotions. It was my way of trying to get back some control in my life and giving you a chance to move on. But it didn't work because I just can't stop loving you Sofia. I should have trusted you more and told you how I felt. That's what I'm doing now… x"

Declarations of love can often be positive and constructive, especially when they're reciprocated and you're in a situation to explore each other's feelings further. But that wasn't the case with Sofia and me. There were two reasons my message led to disaster: Firstly, I was (and still remarkably am) married to someone else. Secondly, Sofia was a former student of mine who had only left the school where I was teaching a few months earlier.

This is the story of my adult life and how relationships and events shaped it in unexpected ways, events that culminated in my inappropriate message. It is a story of education, of love, of illness, of loss, trauma, guilt and grief. It is a story of human frailty and sensitivities, of 'revenge', politics and public humiliation. But above all, it is a story of a psychological search for self-understanding, redemptive healing and truth.

CHAPTER 1

AN ACCIDENTAL TEACHER

"Mary suppressed both a smile and a delightful suspicion
that teaching might not be the worst way to spend the idle
hours between breakfast and society."

Chris Cleave, Everyone Brave is Forgiven

I was, during the twenty-seven years that I did it, an
accident-prone teacher. Not accident-prone in a physical
sense, but in a vocal way. I have always had the ability to put
my foot in it; to say something that will provoke a response
or offend. My intention has never been to hurt anyone, but
I see nothing wrong in playing the devil's advocate and
encouraging people to think outside the box. A truly
effective educator takes you out of your comfort zone.

And I was not just an accident-prone teacher but an
accidental one as well. I did not want to be a teacher as a
child and the thought of becoming one was not something
I entertained. In fact, I rejected the idea of being a teacher
at a relatively young age, mainly because my father, Philip,
was a teacher.

Philip King, was a primary school teacher. Born in Cardiff,
seven years before the Second World War, his childhood
was turbulent, not simply due to that conflict, but also
because his father drifted in and out of different jobs. Philip

changed primary schools four times and secondary schools thrice. Yet, being possessed with a dogged determination and a natural intelligence, he managed to attain his school certificate or 'matriculation'. Armed with that, he had every intention to go to university but his parents were having none of it. They dictated that he had to leave school and get a job, so he found employment doing administration for the British Oxygen Company.

My father progressed from there to doing his national service, and aged twenty, his teacher training. He was a gifted educator with a natural creativity and an understanding of how children learnt. So his career blossomed, leading him to become a headmaster in his early forties.

I had a good relationship with my father but had no wish to follow in his footsteps. I saw at first-hand how much being a headmaster took out of him personally and was aware that the monetary rewards were not, at the time, commensurate with the stress involved. Of course, my father's choice of career did in the end have an influence on me, but the person who gave me my intellectual drive was not my father, but my mother:

My mother, Christine, was born and brought up in Newport, South Wales. She always described herself as an archetypal product of the 1944 Education Act - she passed her 11-plus exam, went to grammar school and then got a grant to go to Exeter university. After a year studying Botany, she transferred to the then fashionable subject of 'Sociology'. Like my father, she was also blessed with a good brain and never missed an opportunity to let people know about it! Both my parents were passionate advocates of state education and social mobility. They understood that a degree from a top university gave people a tremendous freedom of choice and earning potential. So they were determined that all their children would go to a top university. And for them, there was really only one top university – Oxford!

The first to head up to Oxford was my elder sister, Pauline. She read Theology at St Hugh's College. Then three years later, her younger sister Elizabeth gained a place at Worcester College to study Chemistry. Finally, not to be undone by my older siblings, I somehow also talked my way into Worcester College to read History.

All three of us went to the same comprehensive school and none of us is outstandingly academic, so our Oxbridge success was all the more surprising. I suspect it happened due to a combination of luck, determination and self-belief. My father used to say that he gave his children 'the best education that money can't buy.' I disagree – teaching standards at my secondary school were at best average overall and apart from the music department, it gave me little in terms of cultural capital. It was only really when I got to university, that I felt my proper education began. And I was playing 'catch-up' for the lack of a classical and culture-filled schooling.

Another reason that I was an accidental teacher is that teaching was not my first choice of career. I felt from a young age a vocation for the Church of England's ministry. At university, I did everything I could to nurture this vocation, including preaching and singing in my college chapel, and arranging Sunday lunches at the University Church of St Mary's. I garnered enough support to be put forward for a selection conference, which took place in a bleak and cold Durham in January 1987. It was a disaster.

It was entirely my own fault that the selection conference was a disaster. I was, aged twenty, far too immature and lacking in life experience, to cope with the various scenarios and role-play situations. Secondly, I was, and still am, someone who is not very 'clubbable'. I like to be part of a community but I'm not very good at conforming to rules or ways of doing things that make little sense. A selection conference requires one to put on a mask of piety that I just could not manage. I prefer to be myself – challenging and probing others, rather than sitting there agreeing with everything. That's not to say I am disrespectful on a personal level, but that when it comes to ideas and beliefs, they should be constantly re-examined and doubted.

Having failed in my attempt to join the Church as a minister, I had to decide what else I could do with my life. I contemplated doing a gap year working abroad for a charity, and then attempting to reapply for the Church. I still felt a vocation to ordained ministry for a calling never really goes away, but eventually decided reluctantly to enter the family trade and become a teacher as I could not think of anything else to do. I attained a then respectable 'Desmond' (2:2) in my final honours school and gained a place at S. Martin's College, Lancaster to train as a History teacher.

Lancaster was a refreshing change from the rarefied and elitist atmosphere of Oxford. I had enjoyed my time at Worcester College immensely, but three years was enough for me in the 'Dreaming Spires.' My initial confidence and arrogance regarding teaching were soon rubbed off. I went into it with the opinion that 'if my father can do it, then so can I'. After a few weeks' teaching practice in the roughest school in Blackpool, I was thinking, 'how the hell can anyone do this?'

Thus, I had my fair share of 'horror' experiences whilst training to teach. I found myself breaking up fights (in my classroom), having my briefcase stolen and bizarrely, a twelve-year-old girl undressing whilst I was teaching. She was dragged away by some other girls before she became too exposed and I can't remember what happened to her. I was learning the trade and making all the rooky errors that student teachers do such as giving ambiguous and unclear instructions as well as being friendly one moment and then trying to reign it in with a failed attempt at excessive strictness. I was required to write schemes of work, lesson plans and reviews of lessons, but I had little knowledge of the learning process and did not know at first how long activities would take. I was, however, fortunate enough to have an excellent mentor in my Head of Department at the Blackpool school. He was a no-nonsense character on top of his game. Tough but kind, he helpfully pointed out my mistakes and made suggestions as to how I could improve. With his guidance, I scraped through my teaching practice and attained my postgraduate certificate in education. I became what was then known as a 'Probationary Teacher' but is now termed a 'Newly Qualified Teacher'.

Another memory of my teacher training year is the Friday night gatherings in local public houses. I discovered that

Lancaster has several fine hostelries, which my fellow trainee teachers and I enjoyed to excess after a stressful week on the chalk face. This was vital therapy as we told stories of our latest pedagogical cock-ups and laughed off what today would be regarded as 'unacceptable professional conduct'! This was an era when you could be creative and take risks, when you were not condemned for grabbing an unruly kid by his collar, but given tips for implementing better ways of enforcing discipline.

In the spring of 1988 I started applying for teaching jobs. There was a teacher shortage so I had little difficulty getting my first post. I got the second job I applied for, which did not seem at the time a particularly notable success as I was the only interviewee! I was also interviewed for the first position I applied for (in a co-educational Church of England comprehensive school), but on that occasion, there were two of us, and the other person got the job!

The teaching post was at Peterhampton High School, a grammar school for girls aged twelve to eighteen. My first priority was finding a job in a good school and I wasn't bothered whether it was a mixed, boys or girls' school. As it happened, I ended up teaching in a school in which 80 percent of the staff were female, as were 100 percent of the students. In my contract, I was amusingly referred to as an 'assistant mistress' as the school was still using job descriptions created in the 1950's. This was not to be a brave new world of education, but I could see that it could be an environment in which I would be able to develop my teaching skills.

After I got the job, I contacted the school to ask them if they could suggest appropriate and not too expensive rental accommodation. They came straight back with the suggestion of lodging in the downstairs of a fairly substantial detached house on the London Road in Peterhampton, at a remarkably reasonable rent of £150 per month. I jumped at the chance. The owner of the house lived upstairs on her own. Her name was Mrs Ruth Schumann.

Mrs Schumann wanted to meet me before she could agree to my moving in. The property, known as 'Rye Cottage', was a fine example of Edwardian architecture with ceilings, bay sash windows and a stained-glass skylight. The house still had some of its original features including a ceiling mounted laundry drying rack complete with a pulley system in the kitchen.

I arrived at Rye Cottage for the first time on a warm sunny day in June 1988 accompanied by my mother, Christine, and her longstanding friend Pauline, who was only seven years younger than Mrs Schumann. Mrs Schumann talked about herself and the arrangements for living there. She was also keen to find out about me. I discovered that she had celebrated her eightieth birthday the previous month, that she was German, and had fled the Nazi regime in the 1930's. Ruth Schumann was an impressive lady. She was smartly dressed in an outfit that owed more to the 1970's than the late 1980's. Her 70's floral print summer dress seemed entirely appropriate as we ate sponge cake and drank tea from china cups. She was very correct and precise in the way she talked, and laid out the rules of living in her house in an exact manner. I liked her. We were from different generations, with very different personalities, but she was warm and engaging as well as a little bit intimidating.

I started lodging at Rye Cottage on 31st August 1988. Shortly after I moved in, Mrs Schumann informed me that I would be sharing the downstairs of her house with a young French woman. The young woman in question had been appointed as the French language assistant at Peterhampton Grammar School (a boys' school). She was due to arrive at Rye Cottage on Saturday 24th September. Her name was Marie-Hélène Dupont.

CHAPTER 2

MARIE-HÉLÈNE

"The meeting of two personalities is like the contact of
two chemical substances: if there is any reaction, both are
transformed."

Carl Jung

The first thing I noticed about Marie-Hélène when she
arrived on the door step of Rye Cottage was her green
spectacles. I didn't know anyone who wore green spectacles
and was fascinated that this young French woman was
wearing them. But they seemed to work, complementing her
light brown hair. We shook hands, exchanged pleasantries
and then other members of her family started emerging; first
her older sister Béatrice, then her mother, her father, and
finally her younger brother Jean-Paul. I was not expecting
Marie-Hélène to turn up with her whole family, but as it
happened, she had not - there were two other (older)
siblings absent from the party.

It felt at the time a bit like an invasion as I had spent a very
peaceful month at Rye Cottage without having to worry
about anyone else. Most of the time I had been working, but
had made some contacts at the local church. I was fairly
relaxed about this French invasion as they seemed good,
kind people, and I realised that they were there to support

Marie-Hélène and get the lay of the land. They had brought lunch with them – baguettes, paté and salad, and cheese, with boiled eggs and crisps. This invasion was well-organised with nothing left to chance!

Marie-Hélène told me later that her family were quite shocked to see my underpants hanging up on the ceiling mounted drying rack in the kitchen. Frankly, I hadn't thought that she was going to arrive with so many people and had carried on my routine as normal. It was Saturday, which for me was laundry day after having worked Monday to Friday. Now, I can see her point but as a twenty-two-year-old, I was just doing my own thing in blissful ignorance of etiquette.

I was keen to help the new arrival orientate herself, so in the afternoon I showed her Peterhampton with her sister and introduced her to the local supermarket. I gave her a map of the town centre and talked about the few eating and drinking places I had already discovered. I think I overdid it for later she told me that she had found me irritating and had said to her sister Béatrice, "Isn't he going to leave us alone?" To which Béatrice replied, "I think he's just trying to be kind".

By the evening, Marie-Hélène's family had departed and we were left to chat and get to know each other. We prepared separate meals and drank separate wines. Marie-Hélène had just come back from a holiday in Provence and spent the evening sipping one glass of Vaucluse wine. I had spent a tough week trying to educate girls and spent the evening working through a bottle of Chardonnay. She was shocked that I could drink a whole bottle of white wine on my own and still remain cogent. I was surprised that she was not tempted to have a second glass of her red wine. She managed to make that one bottle last two weeks!

We chatted about our families, our education and our recent experiences. I found out that Marie-Hélène was older than she looked. I had assumed she would be my age or younger but in fact she was the grand old age of twenty-five. I noticed that Marie-Hélène was extremely slim, almost anorexic. This concerned me, but I didn't say anything. She, however, was all too aware that she had lost weight and reading my mind, explained the reason for it. In the previous academic year, she had been teaching at a tough Northern French school in Avion (a suburb of Lens). She commuted from her family house in Bruay, but was so nervous about the prospect of teaching the difficult students that she would stop 'en route' and vomit every day.

"If it was that bad, why didn't you just pack it in?" I asked her.

"It was a difficult but also a good experience," she replied, "but I wouldn't want to teach in a school like that again."

She had my respect, for I could see that she was not a quitter. On the contrary, she was one of the most resilient fighters that I have ever met, a quality that she drew upon time and again in future years.

We chatted amicably that first evening and at the end of it I wished her goodnight:

"God bless..." I said as she left for bed. This is not a phrase I have often used. I'm not really a 'god-blessy' type of person. But it seemed the right thing to say that evening. I

17

can only think of one other occasion when I have used that phrase.

*****

Marie-Hélène loved working at Peterhampton Grammar School. After her struggles the previous year, it was a piece of cake. She had been a frontline teacher in a difficult school with a wide socio-economic mix. Now she was at one of the top grammar schools in the United Kingdom working with individuals or small groups consisting of middle-class, polite boys. Furthermore, she was having fun. She got on well with the other language teachers, in particular a young woman called Wendy, who was to become a life-long friend. She was invited on a school trip to France during which she got to know other colleagues, including a young male teacher who took a shine to her:

"He touched my knee while we were watching a film with the students!" she declared. "I was a bit shocked, and had to move his hand away!" I was taken aback that she confided in me.

Meanwhile, I was busy getting to grips with my demanding job at Peterhampton High School. My Head of Department, Janet O'Connor, was a tough taskmaster and I struggled to fulfil her expectations. However, looking back, this helped me to get to grips with the learning process and taught me the importance of a high level of organisation.

On my first day at Peterhampton High School, I found myself in an assembly in which the Headmistress, Mrs Partridge, introduced the new members of staff:

"We have two new members of staff this term," she announced, "Mrs Baker in the Home Economics department and Mr King in the History department."

The sixthformers fell about laughing! I became a History teacher fully aware that 'King' was an aptronym. I have lost count of the number of times people have pointed this out to me. On my passport and driving licence, I am of course King, Charles – it's a bit like a carpet salesperson being called 'Walter Wall'!

The girls at Peterhampton High School were highly intelligent and I made my fair share of mistakes in my first year at the school. More often than I would have liked, the pupils got the better of me. But, at the same time, I was learning from my mistakes and developing good pedagogical skills. It did not help that I was the youngest man in the school by ten years, and there weren't that many men on the staff. I think, in hindsight, I was, as a twenty-two-year-old, an object of fascination for some of the girls. I remember a strange incident at Christmas when a young Science teacher called me out of my classroom and told me to close my eyes. A girl planted a kiss on my cheeks and then rapidly retreated. Such behaviour would be unthinkable today!

In my first term at the school, I was working in the staff room one day when a colleague interrupted me, "Charles, we need your muscle," she said, "a girl has collapsed in the main hall and needs to be taken to matron." I darted into the hall to find a fourteen-year-old semi-conscious, and slumped on the floor, surrounded by concerned colleagues. Three of us bent down to pick her up and I got a heavy whiff of alcohol:

"She's drunk!" I exclaimed with relief. We were then quite happy to pick her up and carry her to matron's in the knowledge that she wasn't epileptic and hadn't suffered any major injury. She had drunk half a bottle of vodka at break time for a reason none of us could fathom. When she had sobered up, the Headmistress hauled her in and suspended her for five days.

Such incidents were very much the exception to the rule at Peterhampton High School. The girls were on the whole well-behaved and after my initial difficulties, I found it a congenial atmosphere in which to teach. Mrs Partridge was an effective headmistress, managing a good balance between firmness and a light touch.

Out of school, I was spending an increasing amount of time with Marie-Hélène. There was nothing romantically happening between us for my interests in that department lay elsewhere. I had three short relationships during my first year at Rye Cottage, but none lasted and I did not sleep with any of them. This was very much a continuation of how I behaved as a student. I would fall in and out of relationships with girls who for one reason or another were not suitable as long-term partners. May be for someone else, but not for me. The last relationship I fell into during my first year at Rye Cottage was with a woman several years my senior. I introduced her to a friend and they got married six months later. I attended the wedding. Within eighteen months of meeting they had a child to whom I became a godparent. I was pleased that it was through me that they had met. I was, in general, pretty naïve about relationships and had never had a long-term girlfriend. When I celebrated my 23rd birthday in March 1989, I was still a virgin.

After her first half-term at Peterhampton Grammar School, Marie-Hélène returned to France for a week and came back with her white Renault 5. It was several years old and had seen better days, but it provided her with wheels, and meant that we could explore the local countryside together. The only issue was that she was a terrible driver. She would drive too fast, too close to other cars, and rarely wore a seatbelt. Her main problem was that she didn't realise one had to stop at zebra crossings. On one occasion I got extremely angry with her for swerving round a man who was a quarter of the way across one. I expressed my displeasure and went into a silent rage. I think she realised what she had done and apologised, yet that was not the last time she almost killed someone.

On that occasion she was driving too fast in Marlow when a girl stepped on to a zebra crossing. "STOP!" I yelled, and with a squeal of the brakes we came to a standstill just inches from her. The girl turned and glowered at us. It was one of my sixth form students! I pathetically and unsuccessfully tried to hide below the dashboard! I ended up mouthing a humble 'Sorry', and then sat there fuming:

"I would prefer if you didn't make attempts at murdering my students," I said to Marie-Hélène through gritted teeth.

I liked the fact that Marie-Hélène was impulsive and go-get-it. She threw herself into British culture and was keen to make the most of her opportunities. She did bed and breakfasting with the Spanish assistant in the Cotswolds, she attended classical concerts with Mrs Schumann and me at St James' Church in Peterhampton, and in the summer she went to Ascot and Wimbledon.

Marie-Hélène didn't tell me she was going to Wimbledon, but proudly presented the programme on her return:

"I saw Boris Becker on Centre Court today," she announced.

"How on earth did you get a Centre Court ticket?" I replied.

"Well, I bought a £5 ticket for the outside courts and then sneaked my way in and sat in an empty chair on the front row. Boris Becker was so close to me at times that I could smell his sweat!"

"But, how did you get past security? And what would you have done if someone had claimed their seat from you?"

"Well I slipped in behind someone else while their ticket was being checked, and you're right, I was afraid that someone would ask for their seat, so I only stayed for about an hour and a half…"

"An hour and a half? You conned your way on to Centre Court and then watched almost a whole match… I tell you M-H, I'm impressed…."

Some people called Marie-Hélène simply 'Hélène', others 'Marie', and of course quite a few people just used all four syllables and called her by her full name. But I came to calling her by the initials M-H, not out of laziness, but because it just seemed right. She liked me calling her that too so 'M-H' stuck.

In July 1989, Marie-Hélène got to the end of her time as a language assistant. Her appointment was only for one year so she was due to leave. On her last night we went out and celebrated her year in England. Afterwards, we started getting physical with each other and one thing led to another. I hadn't wanted to get romantically involved with her whilst we were living together, but as she was leaving the next day, I thought it would not do any harm. However, when I woke up the following morning, I felt guilty for being intimate with her when I knew that she was in love with me, but I wasn't sure that I was in love with her. I suspected she would now go back to France and brood. I had behaved badly and played with her emotions. It did not sit easy with me.

Before she left for France, we kissed and she gave me a little orange piece of paper which I still have today. On it she wrote her name, her address and her telephone number with 'xxx' at the bottom. She obviously wanted me to make the next move and at least phone her that summer. I thought the best thing was to let her get on with her life without me, so I made no attempt to contact her at all.

CHAPTER 3

SOFIA

"But then, no one really got her. No one in the world understood. Hell, if she was honest with herself, not even she understood."

Lacey Alexander

I first met Sofia Messina in November 2008 when she suddenly appeared in my Year 9 'ICT' class. ICT or 'Information Communication Technology' was a subject that I taught as a supplementary subject to my main specialisms of History and Philosophy. Philosophy was an area that I had fallen into during the early 2000's. The ICT syllabus consisted mainly of teaching word processing, spreadsheets, internet research, data protection, social media, and 'staying safe' online. The thirteen-year-old Sofia was a quiet, studious girl who had transferred from another school that November because the journey was more tortuous than the three miles she had to travel to Farlbridge School, a co-educational independent school where I had been appointed as Head of History and Philosophy the previous year. Sofia was a normal looking bespectacled thirteen-year-old girl with medium length brown hair that she kept in a hair band. She seemed a pleasant enough pupil to me – polite and friendly, if a little reserved. She was very well behaved and unlike a lot of the other girls did not attempt to play brinkmanship with the school uniform rules. It is quite normal for teenage girls to push the boundaries by wearing make-up, painting nails and rolling up the tops of their skirts. Sofia did none of this.

I soon ascertained that she was very skilled at ICT. In fact, she excelled at the subject. Later, I found out that she was an only child, and that she was a keen user of social media. I suspect that she honed her ICT skills in the quietness of her bedroom at home.

Apart from her skilled use of ICT, Sofia did not make much impression on me until I became her form tutor the following academic year. She was an isolated girl, and I noticed that after having been in the school for a year, she had not made any close friends. Her mother was concerned about this and rang me to discuss the fact that Sofia was not being accepted into friendship groups. I explained that sometimes it took time for people to develop their confidence in a new school and be part of a friendship group, something I knew from my own experience when I was a school pupil. Like Sofia, I had been socially awkward and it took me two or three years at secondary school to make any friends. However, Mrs Messina seemed concerned that other girls shunned Sofia entirely. She suspected that they actively discouraged others from being friends with her daughter. I said to Mrs Messina that I had not observed that to be the case and promised I would keep an eye on Sofia and let her know if I became aware of any problems.

I also sensed that other girls seemed to be wary of Sofia, or even dislike her, but I had no tangible evidence to back that up so I did not want to exacerbate Mrs Messina's obvious anxiety about her daughter. It also occurred to me that Sofia's peers were just being wary of Sofia as she was different and did not fit in. In any case, I could not understand why anyone would positively dislike Sofia, as I always found her friendly, polite and kind.

During my time as Sofia's form tutor, I not only got to know her, but also her parents. Mrs Francesca Messina was a smart, middle-aged Sicilian woman and a committed Roman Catholic. She told me that Sofia had been a 'miracle' child who had come into the world after she had prayed to St Agatha in the cathedral at Catania. I later found out that Sofia's parents had met when they were teenagers, but they produced their only child in their late thirties. After so many years of trying for a baby, it must have indeed felt like a miracle when Sofia popped into the world. I could not help thinking that producing such a miracle, and being regarded as so special, put a lot of expectations on Sofia. She seemed very keen to please her parents and was under a lot of pressure to succeed.

The first time I met Mr Niccolo Messina was on a school geography trip to the Isle of Sheppey. He was a handsome, slightly bearded, slim man with a dark complexion, who looked rather dapper in his dark green jacket. He was accompanied on the trip by his wife who was also immaculately attired in a brown suit with a white blouse. I thought they were somewhat overdressed for a geography field trip, especially as the summer temperatures were due to reach a balmy 28°celcius that day. They had decided to accompany Sofia on her GCSE geography trip as she suffered from a chronic medical condition. Her condition meant that she had regular medical appointments and in her early years at the school was unable to attend extra-curricular events such as house music and prize-giving. However, Sofia felt confident about attending field trips if her parents were supporting her. I happened to be on the trip as I was good friends with the Head of Geography.

Mr Messina was a successful Sicilian business man in his early fifties who had the confidence of someone who had achieved wealth and responsibility against the odds. He owned an Insurance Company that employed upwards of twenty people and had made some shrewd property investments, the rent from which further bolstered the family's income. I admired him as he was obviously a hard worker who had an ability to adapt to his environment. But what struck me even more than this, was his commitment to his family, in particular, Sofia. And that commitment was not just to her well-being and education, but to her future career. He had plans for his daughter and these plans involved Sofia following in his footsteps. On the Geography field trip, Mr Messina told me that he was looking forward to the day when Sofia took over the company from him, although I had my doubts that this was the right thing for her. It seemed to me that they were putting their business and their ambitions before considerations of what Sofia's gifts and personality were suited to, but Sofia seemed very keen to gain the necessary skills and experience to emulate her father, so it is possible that I was wrong in my assessment. I never expressed my doubts to Sofia or her parents, as it would not have been appreciated.

I asked Mr and Messina why they had left Sicily for the United Kingdom, a country with a much less equable climate. They told me that it was because they could see that there were a lot more business opportunities in the UK. They explained that in Italy tax evasion is rife and although not pervasive, they felt uncomfortable with the influence of the Mafia in Sicily. The Messinas were people of integrity whose religious faith led them to adopt a strong Roman Catholic morality. I admired this, but it also occurred to me that they were a product of a culture in which family ties were all powerful. Perhaps Mr Messina's wish for his daughter to follow in his footsteps, and her willingness to do so, was as much a result of cultural expectations as anything else.

These cultural expectations may also have partly explained Sofia's approach to education. Sofia very rarely missed lessons, as unlike some pupils at the school, she did not take education for granted, but realised how empowering it was. Thus, she was diligent and determined. Her enthusiasm for learning was such, that sometimes she would attend lessons even when she was ill.

Sofia seemed more comfortable around adults than her peers. Perhaps this was because she had older parents with whom she had a very good relationship. She excelled at two subjects – ICT and History. I taught her ICT in Year 9, and then History for GCSE. In the sixth form, she opted to do both History and Philosophy, so I taught her two A Level subjects. I was also her form tutor when she was doing her GCSE's in Years 10 and 11. With few friends in the school, and with a pastorally minded tutor at hand, it is not surprising that it was often to me she turned for support.

Every morning at Farlbridge School, 'Conclave' takes place. Conclave is morning registration involving a house of pupils from Years 9 to 13. In order to register my form pupils during this house registration, I would spot them in a crowded room full of pupils from different year groups. Some of them would give me a wave, but others assumed that they were visible behind strapping six-foot-four sixth formers! The only member of my form who sought me out every morning and exchanged a greeting with me, was Sofia. She would also arrive as early as she could to lessons for a little chat. I found this unusual as it seemed to me that she was more reliant on finding acceptance from me and her other teachers than from her peers, which would also explain why she found it so hard to make friends at Farlbridge School.

I soon came to realise how much my tutee, the fifteen-year-old Sofia, was reliant on me for affirmation at school. One incident crystallised this for me.

The incident I am referring to I shall call affectionately 'Farting-gate'. Of course, it was entirely due to my own mischievous sense of humour that 'Farting-gate' happened. It occurred at lunchtime towards the end of Sofia's Year 10. There were half a dozen pupils in my form room including Sofia and another girl called Taara with whom Sofia had a less than warm relationship. I cannot remember which boy said it, but one of my tutees uttered the words:

"It smells in here!"

"Yes, you're right, it does – what is that smell?" I retorted

"It's Sofia, she's farted!" exclaimed Taara.

"No, I haven't!" protested Sofia.

"It's alright Sofia – don't worry about it – it's a perfectly normal human function," I said with a smirk on my face. I doubted that Sofia had indeed been the culprit but thought it funny to pretend as if she had been. The others laughed and the conversation moved on. Sofia left the room.

Of course, I had got it wrong. I've always been fairly relaxed about farting especially as I do plenty of it myself. However, I had failed to appreciate that other people are much more sensitive about it (particularly self-conscious teenage girls), and are mortified when they are accused falsely or correctly of 'letting one rip.'

Over the next week, Sofia had a face like thunder. She stopped communicating with me and looked at me with total contempt in registration, form time and lessons. For the first couple of days, I thought she was just in a bad mood for some completely unrelated reason, but as her strop continued and she persisted in giving me 'dagger eyes', I came to the conclusion it must have been due to 'Farting-gate'.

After about nine days of this, I realised I needed to apologise to Sofia so that we could draw a line under the incident. So I kept her behind after afternoon registration and said to her:

"I've noticed you've been upset with me over the last week or so. Is it because of my 'farting' comment?"

"Yes, it is, and my mother says that she's thinking of complaining about you...."

"....Look Sofia – you're right - I was out of order, and although I was just trying to be funny, I was very insensitive towards you. I'm sorry."

Sofia visibly relaxed and we agreed to put the incident behind us. She seemed to appreciate my apology, and we reverted to being on friendly terms. The incident made me realise that I had become an influential person in Sofia's life, that she was a very sensitive girl, and that she was not someone that I wanted to upset in the future. I wish I had been thinking more of 'Farting-gate' when a few years later I sent her my inappropriate message!

*****

Shortly after 'Farting-gate', Prize-giving Day took place. Prize-giving was on a Saturday at the end of June and all pupils and staff were expected to turn up. I was required to take a register of all pupils before the morning church service. Sofia had been awarded the Year 10 History prize, not just for attainment, but for her unceasing efforts – she had really worked her socks off. Sofia did not turn up.

I was disappointed that Sofia did not attend Prize-giving, for I thought that getting the History prize would be a real boost for her confidence. However, I could understand why she might have wanted to avoid going up to collect a prize in front of several hundred people.

As I was required to follow up any absentees, I rang Sofia's family before the afternoon prize-giving ceremony. Her mother answered the phone and told me that Sofia was ill when I enquired where her daughter was. I still do not know whether Sofia was ill or not, but I have no reason to disbelieve Mrs Messina; no reason that is except the fact that Sofia had been in school the previous day and was back in school the following Monday.

CHAPTER 4

A CONSCIOUS COUPLING

"Understanding is love's other name"
Thich Nhat Hanh

Opposite Rye Cottage is a large expanse of parkland called 'The Rye' which leads down to a man-made watercourse. In the summer months, there is an open-air swimming pool (a lido) just a few hundred metres from where I lived. During the summer of 1989, I spent a lot of time at the Peterhampton Rye lido. I did not use it during the busy late morning/early afternoon hours, but at the start and end of the day. My interest was in swimming. My father was an excellent swimmer and although I was not as natural an athlete as him, I became a competent swimmer myself.

On the first day of term in September 1989, I was itching to get away from school so that I could fit in a swim before going to the pub for a social. It was a very warm and sunny late summer's day, and my afternoon swim invigorated me. Wendy (Marie-Hélène's friend from Peterhampton Grammar School) had contacted me to tell me that Marie-Hélène was coming back and would be at the pub that evening.

Wendy knew that we had started a relationship, and she was also aware that I had failed to contact Marie-Hélène during the summer. Nevertheless, she was keen to get us back together for there was really only one reason that Marie-Hélène was returning, and that reason was me.

I was both surprised and pleased about the imminent prospect of seeing Marie-Hélène. Being a narcissist, I was flattered that she would leave her country once again to come back to Peterhampton. This time, however, Marie-Hélène had no job and nowhere to live. It was a massive leap of faith to return to the United Kingdom and I am still in awe that she was prepared to take the risk. And I had developed feelings for her. But I knew that if we resumed our relationship it was going to get serious, and I wasn't sure that I could give her the level of commitment that she wanted. So ignoring her and allowing her to move on made a lot of sense in my head.

Of course, Marie-Hélène was massively disappointed with me for not contacting her over the summer. I arrived at the public house and at first, she could barely bring herself to look at me. The word 'awkward' might best sum it up. She was short-tempered with me, tetchy and rude. I understood why, so just took it in my stride. As the evening wore on, a few more drinks were consumed, everyone relaxed and the conversation became more jovial. I made Marie-Hélène laugh and she started to melt a little. By the end of the evening we picked up where we had left off two months earlier. Marie-Hélène was back, and she was back with me.

The main problem for Marie-Hélène was that she had nowhere to live, but Mrs Schumann kindly allowed her to stay at Rye Cottage for three weeks before her new tenant arrived, a French language assistant, called Aurélie. Marie-

Hélène then found a room a few miles down the road. Unfortunately, that didn't work out, so she resorted to knocking on doors until one couple took her in. Meanwhile, I was struggling to get on with the new arrival, Aurélie. She was a perfectly pleasant girl but I think I was too brash for her, and seeing my underpants on the drying rack was for her not only shocking, but unbearable. Half-way through the year Aurélie left Rye Cottage and Marie-Hélène returned. We were back living together, our relationship had settled down, and we were happy. Marie-Hélène found work doing a combination of private tutoring and French language clubs in different towns. She worked not only in Peterhampton, but Amersham and Aylesbury as well. She was not earning a huge amount of money but more than she had as a language assistant, and Marie-Hélène did not need much to live on. She was extremely careful with money.

In the spring of 1990, Marie-Hélène invited me and Wendy to stay with her at her family house in the Pas De Calais. The two most northerly counties or 'départements' in France are the 'Pas de Calais' and the 'Nord'. This region contains towns famous for battles in the first world war including Arras and Lens as well as the city of Lille. On the coast, the ports of Calais and Dunkirk are gateways for British people to explore France and the rest of the continent of Europe. On the west coast of the Pas de Calais you will find the fashionable town of Le Touquet as well as the bustling port of Boulogne and the seaside town of Berck-sur-Mer. Marie-Hélène's family lived about fifty miles from Calais in the ancient county of 'Artois' which occupies the inland area of the Pas de Calais. To the east of the Artois is the town of Béthune where the countryside is mainly flat, but as you move west towards Saint-Pol-sur-Ternoise, it becomes increasingly hilly and picturesque.

Marie-Hélène was born in Auchel, an old coal mining town that declined as the mines shut. Her family lived there until her father bought a plot of land on the edge of the nearby town of Bruay. There he had a large family house built. This is the norm for French people not living in built-up areas. Whereas the British tend to buy a freehold complete with a house and garden, the rural French buy land, and then build a property to their own specifications and needs. This is why there are so many derelict properties in France that are often snapped up by foreigners and renovated. For the native French person, it is often cheaper and more convenient to have a new house built than renovate an old one.

I found Marie-Hélène's family very hospitable and we had a fabulous few days exploring the local area. By this time it was obvious to them that we were in a relationship, so they were not surprised when I came back for a couple of weeks in the summer of 1990. On this occasion, they had Marie-Hélène's eldest sister Collette staying at the house with her three children. Collette was twelve years older than Marie-Hélène. There were nineteen years between the five siblings in the family. Collette was the oldest, Jean-Paul the youngest and in between there was André, Béatrice and Marie-Hélène in order of age. As there was little space left for me in the main house, I ended up in the office. Marie-Hélène's father was a chartered accountant who ran his own small business in an office that he had built adjacent to the home. Like a lot of French businesses, the office was closed for the whole of August whilst he, and his employees took their summer break. So, I bedded down amongst the staplers and filing cabinets, and had use of the office loo. It was hardly luxury, but I was grateful to Marie-Hélène's family that they were prepared to put me up when their house was so full.

By my third year at Peterhampton High School, I was beginning to get into a comfort zone. I had put a lot of work into preparing resources, eliminated a lot of my previous rooky errors, and had become a settled member of the team.

Meanwhile, Marie-Hélène returned to France in the summer of 1990 as she had gained a position as an English teacher at Collège Sainte Thérèse in Saint-Omer. In France, a 'collège' covers what in the United Kingdom would be described as Years 7 to 10, so her youngest pupils were eleven and the oldest were fifteen. After leaving the collège, students then go on to do their baccalauréat at a lycée, which is the equivalent of a British sixth form college apart from the fact that a lycée includes Year 11, as well as Years 12 and 13.

Marie-Hélène fitted in very well at Collège Sainte Thérèse. It was a Catholic school and had a strong cultural identity. The school had an excellent choir and I was impressed by the singing when I attended a concert there. Singing had for several years been an important hobby of mine. At Oxford I had sang in Worcester College chapel choir for three years, in Peterhampton I sang in the Peterhampton Choral Society and for St James' church. I was nowhere near a professional standard, but as an amateur, I held my own as I growled the bass line.

I missed Marie-Hélène during my third year at Peterhampton High School and came to the conclusion that we had a long-term future together. We saw each other in the holidays, and during term-time I would write to her every day. Mrs Schumann became quite alarmed at the size of my telephone bill as in those days ringing France from a landline was considerably more expensive than it is today. I was also growing out of Peterhampton High School. I had learnt a lot but I did not see myself as becoming one of the many long-term members of staff. There is a danger that you become part of the furniture when you have been doing a teaching job in a good school for a few years. The thought of moving on does not hold much appeal. However, I felt that for me it was time to move on. I had a sense of wanderlust. And it seemed obvious that there was only one place to go. Marie-Hélène had spent two years in England, so we decided it was my turn to go to France.

I bought a diamond ring with twin sapphires and presented it to Marie-Hélène with Champagne and packets of crisps! I think I caught her by surprise, but she seemed happy enough and accepted my proposal of marriage. The ring was to my relief a perfect fit. I was twenty-five and she was almost twenty-eight. We were officially engaged to be married.

*****

The town of Béthune lies 21 miles west of Lille. It has a population of about 25,000 inhabitants and its main square is dominated by a belfry that stands 47 metres tall. There is a certain charm about the town centre of Béthune with its sprinkling of bars and brasseries intermingled with an eclectic mixture of shops. I always felt at home in Béthune which is just as well because that is where Marie-Hélène and I lived together when I moved to France in 1991. We rented a one bedroom third floor flat overlooking the beautiful public gardens. We were close to the town centre, just a ten-minutes' walk to the railway station and an eighteen minutes' drive from her family.

I got a job as an English teacher at the Centre Pratique des Langues Étrangères (CPLE) in Lille. I was a 'vacataire' which would equate to a part-time worker on a zero hour contract today. The hours varied from week-to-week so I kept a diary to remind me where I needed to be at any given moment. Most of my students were adults which was for me a very different experience from working with children. There are pros and cons of teaching adults rather than children. On the plus side, adults are generally polite, well-behaved and don't bully their classmates. On the negative side, adults don't normally do their homework and often don't turn up for lessons at all. They then expect you to help them play catch-up once they have come back from a three-week holiday in Guadeloupe. You cannot ring their parents to express concern about their effort and progress, so effectively you have no ability to put pressure on them if they are underperforming. Adults don't surprise you with their rawness, their prejudices and their lack of life experience. They have less 'wonder' of the world and are more cynical! But on the other hand, they get your jokes, they appreciate your efforts to make the learning fun, and play along with it rather than trying to subvert it. You can take more risks with adults.

After eighteen months in France, I decided to return to England. I had gained valuable experience of the country and its language, but the job was not going anywhere. I had no money nor career prospects in France, and I came to the conclusion I enjoyed school teaching more. It was time to resume my career in the UK.

In 1993, there was not the teacher shortage that had existed in 1988, but I did manage to find a short-term contract covering a maternity leave in Godalming near to where my parents lived. It gave me a foot in the door and provided a springboard for other positions later.

Back in France, Marie-Hélène was continuing to enjoy her work at Collège Sainte Thérèse, and although we were apart, our relationship was strong, and we were as committed to each other as we had ever been. Life was good, and I was confident that I could persuade Marie-Hélène to live in England once we got married. But, then, in the summer of 1993 our happiness was shattered by bad news.

CHAPTER 5

SECRET-SANTAGATE

"And why is it, thought Lara, that my fate is to see
everything and take it all so much to heart?"

Boris Pasternak

By the time Sofia got into Year 11 at school, she was
beginning to make friends. She became good pals with a girl
called Lucy, who was academically more able than her but a
bit naïve and eccentric. However, Sofia was still struggling
to be accepted by the majority of her peers. One incident in
particular summed this up:

It was the last day of the Autumn term in December 2010.
My Year 11 form were just a few months away from doing
their GCSE examinations. We had arranged as a form to do
a 'Secret Santa' which involved each person randomly
pulling a name out of a hat (or an empty biscuit tin in this
case). The name chosen was to be the person for whom you
bought and wrapped a present. Everyone, including me,
would have taken part although I cannot recall either what
I received or what I gave as a present on this occasion.

During a form period leading up to the end of term
Christmas service, we all received a present anonymously
from our secret Santa, however, as is the way of these things,
most of the pupils had found out who their present-giver

was. I was not paying much attention to what was going on in my form and was in a laid-back mood. It did not strike me as significant when Sofia came up to me and asked to go to the toilet. I mumbled something like 'no problem', she left the classroom and did not return. I was so inattentive that I forgot she had gone to the loo and was absent.

As the form period came to an end, the Head of House, Daniel Bennett came to see me and asked me if I was aware of what had happened with the Secret Santa present exchange and Sofia. I admitted that I had no idea, and then he told me that Sofia's parents had turned up to the school and asked to speak to the Headmaster. He told me that apparently a boy in the form had thrown an empty chocolate packet at Sofia for her secret Santa, which made her feel humiliated. Her feeling of injustice was exacerbated by the fact that she had bought another pupil a lovely present and wrapped it carefully. She had gone to the toilet in a highly emotional state and phoned her parents in floods of tears. Hence, their appearance at the school.

I said I would investigate. Shortly afterwards, with all the other pupils having gone off to the end of term Christmas service, Sofia turned up, and I asked her what had happened. I made notes, as she explained the incident. It seemed to me that the boy in question had been egged on by others in the form to belittle Sofia, and I could not help thinking that the lad (called Mark) had acted out of character. He was one of the brightest and most responsible members of my form and was due to receive a commendation at the end of term house assembly later that morning.

The Head delegated the incident to Daniel who organised a meeting involving himself and me with Mr Messina, Mrs Messina and Sofia. It was Mr Messina who was the most angry and forceful as we apologised on behalf of the school and the form.

"We will talk to Mark and make it clear to him that this sort of behaviour is not acceptable," said Daniel.

"In addition, he will not now be commended at the house assembly. And we'll make sure that Sofia gets the present that's due to her."

"He should be named in front of the whole house," declared Mr Messina angrily. "He has humiliated Sofia, so he should be humiliated too."

I was alarmed by Mr Messina's vengeful attitude although I knew he was just being emotional about and protective towards his daughter. I said simply:

"We don't do public humiliation at Farlbridge School, Mr Messina."

After the meeting, Sofia went home with her parents whilst Mr Bennett and I talked to the offending pupil. Daniel explained to Mark that he would not now be receiving a commendation at the house assembly, and told him that he would need to buy Sofia an appropriate present to make up for his behaviour. I found myself being unusually emotional, and for the first and last time in my career started to cry in front of a pupil.

"We now have a very unhappy member of the form who has had to go home early. This is not the way we should be ending the term," I sniffled.

My tears and emotions were obviously infectious, as the boy then started crying himself, and showed genuine remorse for what had happened. He promised he would apologise to Sofia and buy her a suitably good present.

After the house assembly I saw my form for a few minutes and told them off, expressing disappointment at the way they had treated Sofia. I was expecting them to be contrite about the whole incident so was surprised when a few of them said that Sofia had blown the whole thing out of proportion and was just being precious. From my point of view, they were being unnecessarily spiteful, but some of them just could not see it.

As I prepared to go home that day, I reflected on what had happened, disturbed not so much by the incident itself, but by the fact that I had cried in front of Mark. I had never wept in front of a pupil before, and it bothered me that I had let my emotional guard down. 'Why did I do that?' I thought to myself, 'Am I just tired and emotional at the end of term or is there something else going on?' I did not understand the reason for my crying but wondered whether it might have been due to something about Sofia, even if I could not put my finger on what it was.

On another occasion shortly after 'Secret-Santagate', a girl started bullying Sofia for apparently no reason. Sofia came up to me and told me that Hannah had come up to her in the girls' toilets and said:

"You're a fuck you are – you're fucking awful, you fuck!" She told me that this had not been the first time that Hannah had verbally abused her. I was surprised by Hannah's behaviour as although she was a little non-conformist when it came to rules, I had never seen her be nasty to anyone. I discussed with Sofia what we could do about it, saying:

"Well, there are two ways we can deal with this. Either we go for the nuclear option and I pass it up to Mr Bennett, we get parents involved and she gets severely punished, or I can have a quiet word with Hannah and I will fire a shot across her bows, telling her that if it happens again, she'll be in big trouble. What do you think?"

Sofia chose the latter option, so I found Hannah that day and had a chat with her. To my relief, Hannah was totally honest about her behaviour. Yes, she had been nasty to Sofia in the loos and yes, she did realise that she should not have done it. Yes, she did understand that it was unacceptable and she would make sure it didn't happen again. Hannah was true to her word and the bullying stopped.

I was rapidly becoming Sofia's fixer and protector. If she had a problem with work, she would come to me. If she had a problem with another teacher or another subject, she would approach me. I was adept at solving problems without making a drama, so I was able to help Sofia. I knew that a quiet word solved most things. I am a strange mixture of astuteness and naivety. On the one hand, I know how to manage things and people, and on the other hand I often underestimate just how malevolent others can be, as I do not wish anyone harm myself.

When Sofia was in the sixth form at school, I continued to support her as best as I could even though I was no longer her form tutor. Every morning she continued to come into the house area and greet me, often sitting down next to me for a little chat. She had also found social acceptance. By the time she was doing her AS Levels, Sofia was part of a small group of girlfriends with whom she felt comfortable. She was gaining in confidence, not only with them, but with me.

CHAPTER 6

FOUR FUNERALS AND A WEDDING

"She was a girl who knew how to be happy even when she was sad. And that's important—you know."

Marilyn Monroe

Maurice Dupont was born in 1925. He was a man of integrity, warmth and generosity. He had worked hard to qualify as a chartered accountant and took the risk of starting his own business. It had paid off for his family had a good standard of living. I admired him greatly and was nervous when I asked him whether I could marry his daughter. At the time, in spring 1991, my French wasn't very good and I said to him:

"Je voudrais mariser votre fille."

The verb 'mariser' doesn't exist in French and I should have used either the verb 'epouser' or 'se marier'. Marie-Hélène was listening from another room and was amused and touched by my grammatical error.

Maurice listened to me with respect and then said simply, "On vas voir", which was a non-committal, "we shall see." I would have preferred if he had said something like, "I'm delighted for both of you," but he was a modest and understated man, so his response was a sincere reflection of how he felt. He certainly did not want to put obstacles in our way, but he also knew that his daughter marrying an Englishman was not going to be easy. I suspect he wasn't sure that I was the right man for Marie-Hélène.

By 1993, my French was fluent and I remember a conversation I had with Maurice in May of that year after he had finished work one day,

"Did you have a good day?" I asked him.

"There are no good days anymore," he replied.

"So why don't you retire? Most men of your age are spending their time in the garden or playing golf."

"I would like to, and there is a chap interested in taking over the business, but I don't know; I'm not sure about him."

I could see that he was depressed, stressed, and weighed down by his responsibilities. He was sixty-eight and had had enough. I told Marie-Hélène and other members of the family that they had to find a way for Maurice to retire. Of course, it was not a simple situation and I don't think my intervention was appreciated. Indeed, it was not my place to interfere. But, I was so concerned about him that I could not help saying something.

In July, he was in the process of shutting his business for the summer break when he fell ill. First of all he had problems with his teeth and then dizziness. He then started having problems with his balance and his speech. He was admitted to hospital. His doctors were not overly concerned about him and diagnosed a mild stroke. All I remember is that he came out of hospital a good deal worse than when he went in. He could hardly walk or speak.

A few weeks later he had a second stroke and was rushed back into hospital. Marie-Hélène and I were the first to arrive at the Intensive Care Unit and were met by a sombre doctor:

"He's not responsive. If he gets worse, do we have permission to turn his life support off?" inquired the consultant. Marie-Hélène burst into tears and even I was shocked by the doctor's directness.

"This is my father you're talking about," she said, "I don't want him to die."

Shortly afterwards, the rest of the family arrived and we went in to see him. There were wires and tubes everywhere; a surreal sight for those of us unfamiliar with procedures in an intensive care unit. Marie-Hélène's brother, Jean-Paul, took his father's hand and said loudly:

"Papa, serre ma main!" ["Dad, squeeze my hand!"]

Maurice squeezed his hand. Jean-Paul repeated the instruction and Maurice responded again. Then Maurice's wife Sophie took his hand and he squeezed her hand too. It was clear to all of us that Maurice was very much there - his consciousness and intelligence were intact.

By the next morning, Maurice had improved further and within two weeks he was back home. He could not walk and struggled to speak at all, but he did improve a little with physiotherapy. It was frustrating for him as he was perfectly aware of everything going on around him but could not communicate properly. He required round-the-clock care.

Once Maurice became ill, he was the focus of attention for all of his immediate family, including Marie-Hélène. I knew it would be difficult for her to leave France with her father incapacitated, so initially I accepted that she needed to be near to her Dad. Any wedding ideas we might have had were very much on hold.

*****

After working in Godalming, I managed to find a temporary appointment in St Albans. It was only for two terms, but it meant I could get away from my parents with whom I had been living for seven months. I lodged with a fellow teacher who I knew from university. She had bought a flat and wanted a lodger to help her pay the mortgage. We got on well, with her showing a lot of tolerance of my various foibles and habits.

In February 1994, my grandmother became seriously ill, so I went over with my parents to see her in a Cardiff hospital. She was eighty-five and had been a creaking door all my life. She had suffered from angina for many years, but when we arrived, she was bent double in pain with osteoporosis. She was also suffering a severe infection. After talking to her briefly my father became distraught to see the state of his mother so withdrew to have a weep. I was more angry than anything else, so went to the nurses' station and said:

"Surely in this day and age it is possible to give someone proper pain relief. Can't you see how much she's suffering?"

The nurse looked at me awkwardly and said hesitantly, "Yes, we're going to get the pain team in on Monday."

"Monday!" I exclaimed, "she's in excruciating pain now – it's not right that she's left in this state."

When I saw her again a week later, she was drugged up, comfortable and drifting in and out of consciousness. She had deteriorated, but there was a serenity and calmness that reassured me. She died twelve hours later.

My father was naturally upset at her death and cried in front of me, "I'm never going to see her again," he mumbled. There was nothing I could say.

My father's brother, Jim, and his wife, Margaret lived with my grandmother in Cardiff. They organised the funeral and hosted a wake afterwards at their house. There is nothing more poignant or emotional than revisiting someone's house after they have died. Often it is the small things that get to you, such as a dressing gown left on a chair, a half-finished crossword or the remnants of a gin bottle left in the fridge. And so it was the familiar smell of my grandmother's room with her furniture and photographs that made her death real to me.

Less than two years after she died, another member of the same household, Margaret, was diagnosed with cervical cancer and died at the age of 56 in May 1996. Once again, we all attended a funeral in Cardiff and a wake at the same house. Uncle Jim struggled to cope without the wife and mother with whom he had lived for decades. In May 1997, he suffered a heart attack and died less than a week later. He was 58. For the third time within the space of three years we attended a Cardiff funeral and a wake at the house, now devoid of the three occupants who had supported each other over so many years. The house was sold shortly afterwards.

In September 1994, I managed to get a permanent post at Banberry Grammar School near Slough. It was the first school I had taught in which felt like 'home'. It was a traditional mixed grammar school led at that time by the old-school patrician headmaster, Dr Nicholas Wilkinson. I liked Dr Wilkinson. Perhaps it was because he was the same age as my father, and like him, there was a decency and compassion about the man which shone out. At my interview, Dr Wilkinson was more interested in my family background and education than how good a teacher I was. He had been Headmaster of Banberry Grammar since 1973, and had moulded the school in his own image, overseeing a growth in numbers as well as an improvement in academic standards. Not everything was perfect about the school, but teachers were given the freedom to get on with the job without too much interference. Hence, when I was made Head of History, I was given a free reign to do what I wanted. My colleagues and I were able to transform a failing department into one that achieved the best results in the school.

As far as work was concerned, everything was coming together. I was becoming an effective manager and enjoying the demands and rewards of being a form tutor. I even thought that perhaps I might have a long-term future at Banberry Grammar School. But, I was becoming increasingly unhappy with the situation I found myself in with Marie-Hélène. By the summer of 1995, it had been two years since her father had fallen ill. His condition had stabilised and she was continuing to enjoy her work at Collège Sainte Thérèse. I did not want to live in France and Marie-Hélène did not seem that keen to move to England. In England I was increasingly living the life of a bachelor, chatting up other women, partying with my friends and going away on walking weekends. Some people I knew were not even aware that I had a long-term partner. The following anecdote illustrates this well:

At lunchtime, during the school day, a group of us used to play cards in the staff room at Banberry Grammar School. Some colleagues thought our behaviour unprofessional and decadent, but we found our half-hour card games a great distraction from the pressures of the job. We would laugh and joke, and became the social hub of the staff room. I was the most raucous and outrageous person in the group, even though it was essentially harmless fun. We would co-opt any new member of staff we could into our card-playing group. One person that we did manage to recruit was a young trainee teacher called Mina.

One day, we were in the middle of one of our lunchtime card-playing sessions, when I casually mentioned something about Marie-Hélène referring to her as my fiancée. Mina suddenly stood up, pointed at me, and exclaimed in astonishment:

"Yoooou've got a fiancée!" [The emphasis of her voice being on the first syllable 'you'].

I was speechless, but my colleagues found it hilarious. It occurred to me that I must have come across as remarkably immature and carefree to warrant her reaction.

I came to the conclusion that I could not continue in a relationship with someone who lived and worked in a foreign country, so I gave Marie-Hélène an ultimatum: either we split up or we get married and she moved to England. Writing it like that, it sounds harsh, for one could argue it should have been me that moved to France. However, logically, our future looked a great deal brighter in the United Kingdom. I was a qualified teacher, Marie-Hélène was not. I was earning quite a bit more money than her. There were a lot more career opportunities for both of us in Britain than France. And, if we were going to buy a house together, it would be a better investment on the outskirts of London than the outskirts of Lille.

Marie-Hélène was not surprised by my ultimatum. She also realised that we could not just continue as we were indefinitely. We had by that stage known each other seven years and been engaged for well over four. I knew it would be difficult for her to leave her family, but it was time for us to make our own.

Marie-Hélène responded to my ultimatum by introducing me to numerous wedding venues so that we could plan our marriage for late July or early August 1996. We looked at cafés, restaurants, hotels, village halls and chateaux. The wedding became a mission for both of us, and it was enjoyable to visit and scrutinise the different venues.

Eventually, we chose the most expensive option and booked Chateau de Rembart near Arras. It had recently opened as a wedding venue; the owners having invested a large amount of money into its renovation. With its grand nineteenth century façade, beautifully built glass dining area, and extensive grounds, we decided that Chateau de Rembart would be ideal for entertaining our guests.

And so it was that on Saturday 27th July 1996, I married Marie-Hélène Dupont. In fact, I married her twice, as in France the tradition is to have a civil wedding at the town hall and afterwards a church wedding. The civil wedding took place at the 'Marie' (town hall) of Bruay. It involved standing before an official who was wearing a sash styled according to the French flag in red, white and blue, and then answering 'Oui' to a couple of legal questions. The most memorable part of this ceremony was when I stood on Marie-Hélène's wedding dress causing a small tear in the train. She looked at me with such annoyance that I thought for a moment she was going to say, 'Non.'

After the civil wedding, we drove a few miles up the road to the church in Camblain-Châtelain to have our religious wedding. It was at this moment that I felt a profound feeling that I had made a terrible mistake. I said to my 'témoin' (witness) Paul:

"So am I officially married now?" I knew what the answer was but was also wondering what would happen if I went AWOL and never turned up to the religious part of our wedding. I loved Marie-Hélène profoundly, but I was not sure that I had done the right thing by marrying her. That ten-minute car journey between the town hall and the church was the most difficult one of my life.

My doubts evaporated once I was in the church and saw the look of happiness on Marie-Hélène's face. The nuptial mass was a moving and happy event. So much so that when Marie-Hélène's disabled father wept loudly, everyone was deeply touched. I had obtained a dispensation from the local bishop for my family and I (who were Anglicans) to take communion at the Catholic wedding. So it felt like not just a union of two people and two families, but also the reunification of two religious denominations that had been rent asunder in the sixteenth century.

Marie-Hélène and I had planned the church service meticulously as we had every other aspect of our marriage. On the wedding day, the focus for her family, however, was more on getting her father ready than it was on her. On the morning of our marriage, she had to drive herself to the hairdressers and sort out last-minute arrangements at the chateau without any help. She told me later how stressful it had all been for her, but she was a perfectionist and wanted everything to run like clockwork. I would have happily assisted her, but we were respecting the tradition of spending time apart the night and morning before our union.

After the church service, we went to the chateau for what is known in France as the 'vin d'honneur'. This is a reception of champagne and canapés for everyone who knows you including neighbours, distant relatives and colleagues. All the cars in the marriage cortege were decorated with ribbons and beeped their horns in the traditional way as we drove the few miles to the chateau. Marie-Hélène was waving and smiling at passers-by. I had never seen her so happy.

The sun came out for our vin d'honneur so it took place outside. Over 150 people attended, and with the wine flowing freely, people soon relaxed, and a jovial atmosphere developed. An impromptu game of football started up, the French and the English finding a common language in the game. It was not just cordial but entente cordiale! During the reception, Marie-Hélène and I were dragged off by the official photographer to do some posed photos. It lasted over an hour and a half and I hated it. In one of them I looked disgruntled, scowling with annoyance at how long the session was going. Marie-Hélène later decided that this was her favourite photograph of me. "It shows your true character!" she opined.

In the evening, ninety family and friends sat down for the main reception - a seven course meal with white and red wines. We hired a disc jockey who also acted as master of ceremonies. At French weddings, not only is music played, but the DJ will also arrange group dances and games. Unlike British weddings there are no speeches, but an ability to mix in and make a fool of oneself is a must. One game involves everyone standing in a big circle with one person in the centre holding a large handkerchief. When the music stops, the person in the middle has to choose someone from the circle to drag to the middle and kiss while kneeling on the handkerchief. Once they have embraced, the handkerchief is passed to the chosen person, who then has to choose someone else to kiss. This continues on and on until virtually everyone has embraced at least one person.

The dancing traditionally starts with a waltz between the bride and groom, which would be great if you could dance, but I cannot. I did contemplate having dancing lessons before the wedding, but as I have absolutely no interest in dancing unless I have drunk a few glasses of wine, I spared myself the effort. Ironically, the one dance I had been taught some fifteen years earlier when at school, was the waltz, so I planted my feet firmly below Marie-Hélène's dress and pretended that I could waltz. We just about got away with it.

The dancing and games and eating went on into the early hours. Eventually, Marie-Hélène and I were able to depart and went to a hotel in Arras for our first night together as man and wife. We were woken next morning by the sound of a radio-controlled farting machine that my friend Matthew had sneaked into our room and placed under our bed. His three-year-old son, Tom was gleefully causing all kinds of disgusting noises from the other side of the door.

Marie-Hélène said afterwards that our wedding day was the happiest day of her life. I also have great memories of it. Yes, I had a wobble between the town hall and the church, but the day was not about me; it was about Marie-Hélène. It was her day, her joy, and we made it happen together.

*****

After we got married, we went to live for a short while in my sister Pauline's flat in Hounslow. This was a stopgap whilst we searched for a house to buy together. Marie-Hélène had been saving for years and had accumulated enough money so that we could put down a 10% deposit on a property. After looking at several places, we eventually found a two-bedroomed house just two hundred metres from Banberry Grammar School. A week after finding the house and having our offer accepted, Marie-Hélène was called back to France. Her father had been taken into hospital.

I did not realise how bad things were until I got a tearful phone call from Marie-Hélène telling me that her father was about to die. I rushed over on a Friday night in October 1996 and spent the weekend observing a rapid decline in his condition. I really felt for Marie-Hélène and her family as they struggled to come to terms with his imminent death. He passed away early the following Monday, and his funeral took place five days later.

The French approach to death is different to the British. First of all, the dead person is normally brought home and laid out in a specially prepared room, so that friends and family can come and pay their respects before the funeral. This is what happened with Maurice – all his immediate and extended family as well as some longstanding friends came to the home and said their farewells to him as he lay in a downstairs bedroom. The only noise was the murmur of the chiller that was left on constantly to keep his body cold. A lot of British people might find this morbid, but I found it both natural and dignified. It also arguably helps the mourning process, as the death of that loved one becomes very real and one can say goodbye in a physical way.

A second difference is that at a Catholic French funeral service, it is the tradition that men and women are separated. Men sit on the right side of the church and women on the left. I found this tradition less easy to understand as I wanted to comfort Marie-Hélène during her father's funeral service but could not.

Losing a parent is not easy, but Marie-Hélène coped with it very well. Besides, we had a lot to do as we started our married life together. In December 1996 we moved into the house we had purchased in Banberry. We were young and healthy, and looking forward to creating a future together. Yet, I had a sense of foreboding, which just wouldn't leave me. I felt that dark clouds were on the horizon. I was not wrong.

CHAPTER 7

AN INFORMAL RELATIONSHIP

"Relationships don't always make sense. Especially from the outside."

Elizabeth Dessen, 'Along for the Ride'

As Sofia approached her AS exams in her Lower Sixth year in 2012, she asked me for extra help with her Philosophy A Level, a subject that she struggled with more than History. I arranged extra lunchtime sessions which she and her friend Lucy would attend. Sofia would also email me from her personal email address asking me for help with specific questions, and I would provide her with sample answers. The tone of her emails were always friendly, asking me whether I was having a good weekend etc. She would often end her emails with a smiley face! I was friendly and helpful in my replies.

As time went on, our relationship became even more informal. It is not unusual for there to be more banter and more informality between teachers and their sixth form pupils in their last year at school. Our relationship was not physical or romantic, but more based on what I thought was a mutual understanding and a shared sense of humour.

This shared sense of humour included an incident that happened in November 2012 when I accidentally sent Sofia's mother a romantic text intended for my wife! My wife was abroad at the time, so I sent her a message enthusing about the latest series of 'Breaking Bad' which she had seen, but I hadn't. My text read as follows:

"Hi babes, Just caught up with the latest episodes of Breaking Bad. It was brilliant – Bryan Cranston is amazing…. Missing you and love you loads, C xxxxx"

I think the reason I accidentally sent the text to Francesca Messina rather than to my wife was because the last text I had received had been from Sofia's mother, thanking me for the support I was giving Sofia! Mrs Messina was one of only a few parents who had my mobile number. She had saved my number to her phone after I had rung her using my mobile one day.

When I realised I had sent this text in error, I was mortified and quickly sent a follow-up message:

"Hi, I think I accidentally sent you a text intended for my wife. Very Sorry, Charles King."

Within a minute I had a reply: "No problem!"

Phew, I was relieved. No harm done and I hoped Sofia had not picked up on my error. If she had done, it occurred to me that she would be ripping it out of me the following day, simply exacerbating my embarrassment. I was not that bothered by it, but it was certainly not something I wanted Sofia's peer group to know about.

The following day, I got to school at my normal time of 8am. As I was about to go into my office, I saw that there was someone sitting in the classroom. It was Sofia. She had some books out and appeared to be working. 'Oh God, she saw my accidental text,' I thought to myself. I did not want to talk about my embarrassing cock-up, but also did not want to appear a coward either. So I popped my head round the door of my classroom and said to Sofia,

"Good morning, you alright?"

"Oh, I'm very well thank you," said Sofia beaming.

It was later on in the day that the subject of my text came up. Sofia was attending a Philosophy lunchtime clinic with her friend Lucy. After a while, she said:

"You made me laugh so much last night with that text to my Mum."

"I thought you might know about that. I know, I'm such an idiot."

"Don't worry about it," said Sofia, "I picked up your text when Mum was in the kitchen. Her phone pinged up with your message and I thought, 'That's weird.' I called to Mum and said, "Mr King has sent you a strange text." Then your second text came through and Mum told me to text back, "No problem," so I did!"

I appreciated that Sofia found the whole thing so funny and I knew her and Lucy well enough to realise that my mistake would go no further. I was grateful to Sofia that she had talked about it in such a way that my embarrassment was extinguished.

Sofia and I were developing a bond of trust, a bond that I later destroyed with my inappropriate message, but which formed around the time of my accidental text.

A week or so later, at the beginning of December 2012, I was doing a lesson on twins as part of the Philosophy 'Ethics' unit. Afterwards, Sofia stayed behind and said to me:

"I was one of twins when I was born. The other one didn't survive."

I was surprised by her statement as she was quite a private person and rarely talked about deeply personal matters.

"I've never told anyone that before," continued Sofia.

I was taken aback - Sofia had confided in me something that she had never told anyone else. This cemented the bond between us and made me feel even more responsible for her.

As we approached Christmas, Sofia told me that she was going to celebrate the festival in Sicily. She said that she did not really want to go as it would involve endless socialising with her extended family. I was sympathetic as I am not a great fan of glad-handing. Although superficially an extrovert, I am happiest walking in the countryside or sitting up in bed drinking coffee. I suspect that most people are the same – it is the simple things in life that give us most satisfaction.

A couple of days before the end of the autumn term in December 2012, we had our last History lesson of the term, which involved an impromptu party with all the members of Sofia's class. It was early in the morning and everyone was relaxed. I remembered the now infamous Secret Santa incident that had happened two years earlier and reflected on how far Sofia had come from there. She was more confident and had found a group of friends with which she felt comfortable. After break on that day, I popped into my office and found a can of diet coke on my desk. I wondered who it might be from. When I checked my school email account, the answer was there:

"Hi Sir, I left a coke on your desk for you :) Sofia"

I was touched by her kindness, so quickly emailed a reply:

"Hi Sofia, Thanks so much — you're such a sweetheart. I was in need of it, and have finished drinking it :) S x"

It is a measure of how relaxed our relationship had become that my reply was so informal. This was reflected in the fact that I sometimes used to end my emails with the initial 'S' as Sofia always used to call me 'Sir' and I cannot remember a single time she ever addressed me directly by my surname as most pupils did. 'S' was short for 'Sir.' I reasoned at the time that my reply was a fitting response to a thoughtful gesture. Often it is the small things that move you, rather than grand gestures.

The day after my 'such a sweetheart' email, Sofia gave me a bottle of Macallan whisky. I gave to her and her parents bagels that I had baked myself. Mrs Messina had made a habit of baking me Sicilian biscuits, so I reasoned it was time for me to show off my culinary skills!

The evening before flying off to Sicily for Christmas, I was not surprised when Sofia emailed me, asking me for sample answers for her studies and complimenting me on my bagels. I replied with a jokey email and wished her and her family an enjoyable Christmas. In return, Sofia wished me and my family a Happy Christmas.

Before we returned to school after Christmas, Sofia and I sent each other a couple of emails. On one of them, Sofia harked back to my 'such a sweetheart' comment by saying that I was 'such a gem', to which I replied that she was 'such a wit.' I was glad that she had appreciated my 'such a sweetheart' email and was able to joke about it.

Sofia was approaching her eighteenth birthday and I was acutely aware that she was under a lot of stress with her A Levels coming up and trying to cope with a difficult medical condition. I knew that the next six months would be crucial to her future and was determined that I would give her as much support as I could.

CHAPTER 8

MASS

"Be unprepared, that's my motto. Be unprepared, and let
life overwhelm you."

Marty Rubin

The first year of my marriage to Marie-Hélène proved to be
difficult for other reasons apart from the death of her father.
One significant event was when she missed her period and
we were hopeful that she might be pregnant. Before we
whipped up the courage to do a pregnancy test, she started
bleeding heavily, which we suspected was an early
miscarriage.

There were, however, other issues that we needed to
confront. I had to adjust to the fact that I was a married
man, and Marie-Hélène had to adjust to the prospect of
living with me permanently in the UK. In fact, she had been
spending an increasing amount of time not with me, but
with her family in France. At one point we were apart for
eight weeks. Her father had died, and she wanted to be there
for them, but it seemed to me that she was over in France
too much. If we were to make a success of our marriage, we
had to spend a lot more time together. Marie-Hélène agreed,
so it was a relief when, in September 1997, she got a part-
time job teaching French at a local school near Banberry. It

was only for a year, but I was pleased that she was earning money and getting herself involved in the community.

However, by the summer of 1998 things were deteriorating between us again. We were arguing a lot, Marie-Hélène was getting increasingly irritable and I was beginning to wonder whether we could sustain the marriage for much longer. Just before I broke up for the summer holidays in July 1998 I was playing as wicket keeper in the staff cricket team when I injured my knee badly and ended up in Accident and Emergency at Wexham Park hospital in Slough. I had had key hole surgery on the same knee the previous year so volunteering to keep wicket had not been a wise choice. I was embarrassed to be taken by ambulance to the hospital, but I was in agony, and the school was taking no chances.

Normally, Marie-Hélène and I would go camping during the summer holidays, but as I was on crutches, we opted instead to rent a chalet in the Alpes. We had a good holiday, but Marie-Hélène started getting headaches and toothache. She was also becoming increasingly irritable. We went to a dentist and she was diagnosed with an abscess on a tooth. They gave her antibiotics and then removed the offending tooth. When we got back from holiday, she remained very moody, continued having headaches and was concerned by the irregular periods she had been having for the previous six months. She went to see her doctor, explained all her symptoms, and the doctor suggested she was being neurotic. I was surprised that our GP had been so direct with Marie-Hélène, but we knew the doctor socially, so perhaps she felt a little less inhibited with us.

By September 1998, Marie-Hélène's headaches started to increase in frequency, so she contacted the newly created NHS direct who suggested she see her GP again.

On the evening of Wednesday 23th September 1998, Marie-Hélène went to bed early with a bad headache. I stayed up to watch football. When I went to bed at about 10.30pm, Marie-Hélène was lying on her back in the bed with her eyes open. I started talking to her but she was not responding. I became increasingly angry and frustrated, thinking that she was trying to wind me up. After a while, she started speaking quietly, seemingly completely oblivious to anything I had said to her. She then told me that she thought she had wet herself. I changed the sheets and I talked gently to her, realising that there was something wrong with her. I said a prayer out loud asking God to look after her. This seemed to reassure her. We both then went to sleep.

The next day I got up and reflected on the previous evening. As I shaved, I wondered whether I had dreamed it, but knew that it was real. Marie-Hélène was not well and I needed to get her to a doctor soon. I resolved to talk to her about it later in the day. I dressed for school, made my sandwiches and prepared to leave the house.

Suddenly, I started hearing a banging noise from upstairs accompanied by rapid breathing. I rushed upstairs to see Marie-Hélène frothing at the mouth and shaking violently. This went on for about two minutes. I rang 999 and asked for an ambulance. I was hyperventilating from shock. They told me to put her in the recovery position and assured me that the ambulance would arrive shortly. So, whilst still covered by the duvet, I tried to move the top half of her body clockwise, placing her head on top of the back of her left hand. She was completely out of it, but I sat there, stroking her hair, and trying to reassure her. She mumbled quietly, "J'ai peur" [I'm scared]. Later, she told me that she had no memory of saying this, but her words moved me to try to reassure her further – "Je t'aime Marie-Hélène; Ne t'inquiete pas - l'ambulance va arriver bientôt."

It was 25 minutes before the ambulance arrived. I don't know why it took so long as the hospital was only four miles away. Perhaps my call had been deemed a low priority. It was rush hour, so they would have encountered traffic. But they had a siren to get through that. Whilst I was waiting for the ambulance, I rang work to say that I would not be in, and then stayed with Marie-Hélène, who was taking a long time to regain full consciousness.

It was both comical and a little surreal when the ambulance men did eventually arrive. Marie-Hélène had only just regained her faculties and looked at them, saying, "What are you doing here?" She had two strangers and me peering over her and did not have a clue what had happened. They were very professional, calmly telling her why they were there. They explained that they would be taking her to hospital and adjusted the duvet to move her. This was embarrassing as she was naked from the waist down, having wet the bed the previous evening. She had wet it again. They withdrew, whilst I sorted out some clean pyjamas for her. She was just about able to walk, so rather than using a stretcher down our steep staircase, they supported her weight and helped her to the ambulance.

On the way to the hospital, the ambulance man tried his best to be reassuring. Most medical professionals are incredibly kind and caring, exhibiting great empathy. And, John, as he introduced himself to us, was no exception. "Don't worry, they're just going to do a few tests," he said to Marie-Hélène, "It's probably just a one-off," John continued. His calmness and humanity relaxed both of us.

At the hospital Marie-Hélène was put on a trolley and transferred to a side room in the Accident and Emergency department. A doctor came to see her and examined her quickly. He then asked a female colleague to look at her. Marie-Hélène was not well. She was vomiting and still had a headache. It did not look good, and I was very concerned. I had a strong suspicion what I thought was wrong with her, as I started to piece together all her recent symptoms in my mind.

The way someone looks at you often communicates more than words could ever manage. Sometimes you see love in a face, other times confusion, anger, fear or curiosity. A lot of the time a face is deadpan, disinterested or apathetic. But the way the woman consultant looked at me after examining my wife was very telling. She had asked Marie-Hélène to stick out her tongue, which appeared severely bruised from the seizure she had had earlier. She had bitten it badly. The doctor was also aware that Marie-Hélène had no history of epilepsy. She looked at me with deep concern. Not a word was spoken between us; there was no need. From that point onwards, I knew we were in trouble.

The hospital arranged a Computed Tomography (CT) scan of her head for later on in the day, so Marie-Hélène and I were left on our own for a lot of the time. She improved a little, and I asked her whether she wanted me to tell her family what had happened:

"They will come straight over if I tell them," I said.

"That's what I want – I want to see Maman," she replied.

Neither of us had mobile phones, so I found a public telephone and rang my sisters first. My sister Pauline offered to pick up Marie-Hélène's mother from Dover and my sister Elizabeth said she would come over after work to support me. I then rang Marie-Hélène's mother to explain what had happened. She was tearful and pledged to come over that day with Béatrice, Marie-Hélène's sister. Arrangements were in place.

At one point, I wandered into the corridor and bumped into an ambulance man who recognized me, "I know you," he said, "Cricketer! We brought you in a few weeks ago!" In normal circumstances I would have found this funny and joked with him, but my sense of humour had abandoned me. I explained that this time I was in the hospital because of my wife.

In the afternoon, I ironically had a long-planned appointment in the physiotherapy department of the same hospital, which was a follow-up to my knee injury. My appointment took place coincidentally at the same time as Marie-Hélène had her CT scan. The physiotherapist looked at my knee, asked me to do a few movements, and then declared that I had made remarkable progress and did not need to see her again. I could not have cared less – there were more important things on my mind.

By 6pm, Marie-Hélène had been in A&E for nine and a half hours. A consultant approached me and ushered me out of our side room into the corridor. He put up the results of the CT scan and said:

"You see this mass on the right frontal lobe of her brain?"

"Yes," I replied, open mouthed. It was impossible not to see it, as before me was a white area roughly the size of a golf ball.

"That's the problem."

"This is not good," I heard myself mumble.

"This is as bad as it gets," came the reply.

I swallowed hard and stared aimlessly into space, numbed by the news.

We discussed what it might be and he said it could be an abscess on the brain as I had already indicated she had suffered from an abscess on a tooth during the summer. It was possible the infection had spread from the jaw into the brain.

"Alternatively, it could be a brain tumour," he explained. "Only a Magnetic Resonance Imaging (MRI) scan will tell which it is."

"If it's an abscess, she will need to be operated on straight away," he continued.

"I hope it is," I replied, for the alternative filled me with despair.

"Whichever it is, there's some urgency about this. She's going to be transferred to either the John Radcliffe in

Oxford or Charing Cross hospital in London as soon as possible. They both have great neurological departments and she'll be in good hands. In the meantime, we'll admit her to a ward."

Marie-Hélène was given a proper bed in a ward almost twelve hours after arriving in hospital and shortly after my sister Elizabeth had arrived. Visiting hours were coming to an end, so I had no choice but to leave her. Elizabeth gave me a lift home and we managed a bite to eat. However, I was called back to the hospital at 9.30pm. Marie-Hélène was being transferred to Charing Cross Hospital.

For the second time that day, I found myself in an ambulance, but this time they had the siren on and red lights were being jumped. I found this reassuring for it meant that they thought Marie-Hélène had an abscess on the brain and needed emergency surgery. As soon as we arrived at Charing Cross they put her in surgical stockings in preparation for an operation, and took a sample of blood to be tested. Marie-Hélène's mother and Béatrice arrived at about 1am in the morning. It was an emotional moment for all of us. We eventually got home at 3am.

I still regard Thursday 24th September 1998 as the most traumatic day of our life together. There would be other difficult days and other traumas to come, but for me that day stands out as a shocking and pivotal moment; our lives were turned upside down. For Marie-Hélène, nothing would ever be the same again.

CHAPTER 9

DIAGNOSIS AND TREATMENT

"The question is not how to get cured, but how to live."

Joseph Conrad

I woke up the next day distraught. I am not someone easily moved to tears, but I wept loudly. Béatrice heard me and comforted me. I was bereft that this was happening to us and had a thought that it was my fault Marie-Hélène was ill. I had slept just three hours, was still in shock from the previous day's events, and my emotions were overwhelming me. However, after a couple of mugs of strong coffee and some breakfast, I was ready to face the day.

I drove Sophie (Marie-Hélène's mother) and Béatrice to Charing Cross hospital. I was glad of the company. When we arrived at the hospital, Marie-Hélène was still in her surgical stockings but they seemed in no hurry to operate on her. I asked to speak to a doctor:

"My understanding was that she might have an abscess on her brain and would need an emergency operation," I said.

"Well, we've done blood tests and they don't seem to indicate that it is an abscess," replied the doctor.

"Okay, so what next?"

"We've booked her in for an MRI scan, so that should help us with a diagnosis."

I accompanied Marie-Hélène to the MRI scan. The hospital had given her some steroids which had perked her up. She seemed remarkably chipper. Marie-Hélène was impressively brave. An MRI scan of the brain requires the patient to go head-first into a tunnel, keeping their head completely still. A series of loud magnetic thuds, a bit like a slow-motion hydraulic drill, continues for twenty-five minutes until a map of the brain is created.

Marie-Hélène closed her eyes, and somehow managed to block out both the noise and the claustrophobia many people feel in this situation. Headphones that play soothing music help the patient, but nevertheless, it is easy to panic. The patient is given a panic button in case they do feel overwhelmed, but Marie-Hélène did not use hers.

I was full of respect for the way Marie-Hélène coped with what was happening to her. Not only was she able to block out the discomfort of an MRI scan, she was able to block out anything negative:

"I don't want to know too much detail," she said to me later, "All I need to know is how they're going to treat me." She had realised by this stage that it was most likely a brain tumour, but did not want to mention the 'c' word. She certainly did not want to know a prognosis, nor any technical, medical details of her condition. Her mother was the same: Keep it simple, don't mention cancer, and let's get on with solving the problem.

I was the complete opposite. I was already searching the internet for every bit of information I could get on brain tumours, however, my limited medical knowledge meant I was struggling to get my head round the different possibilities. I knew that there was a grading system for brain tumours from one to four. A Grade 1 was less likely to come back, a Grade 3 was faster growing, and a Grade 4 was the worst of all. I also found out that with improvements in treating leukaemia, brain cancer was becoming the most common cause of death amongst young people. Of course, Marie-Hélène was not technically a young person, but at thirty-five, was far too young in my mind to be going through this ordeal.

When, a few days later, the diagnosis did come, it was bad news. Marie-Hélène's consultant, Nigel Mendoza, took me aside and put up the results of her MRI scan, showing me a more detailed image than her first CT scan.

"This is what we call a grade 4 astrocytoma," he explained.

"Okay, that diagnosis sounds bad. Can you be absolutely sure you've got it right?"

"Well I'd say, we can be about 95% certain, but we will need to do a biopsy to confirm the diagnosis. That involves putting a needle in her brain and taking a sample. There are risks to the procedure but they are minimal."

"And then what?"

"Given its position, it would not be easy to operate on, so we'll be giving her radiotherapy."

"So what is the prognosis?" I asked.

"The average survival rate is about eighteen months, about 15% of people live two and a half years, and 5%, five years."

I tried to process the information but all I could think was 'Shit, my wife's fucked – she's going to die.'

I was upset and found myself saying,

"But she's only 35, I'm only 32. We're too young to be going through something like this."

Mr Mendoza was sympathetic and was able to combine a straight forward, factual approach with a human warmth.

"Yes, it's tough," he said, "I gave the same diagnosis to a seventeen-year-old girl last week."

I found it comforting, to know that there were other people, in some cases even younger than Marie-Hélène, going through the same plight, even though I did not want to contemplate their suffering.

"So what are we going to tell Marie-Hélène?" inquired Mr Mendoza.

"She doesn't want to know too much detail. Obviously, she needs to know that she has a malignant brain tumour, but she doesn't want to know any technical details or how long she's going to live. The main thing she wants to know is what you're going to do, to treat her."

I went back to see Marie-Hélène, who was sitting up in bed:

"You look upset," she said to me, "As if you've been told something bad. What's wrong?"

"No, I'm fine," I lied. "Mr Mendoza just wants to have a chat with us to talk about treatment options."

Shortly afterwards, Nigel Mendoza called us into his office and sat us down. He explained to Marie-Hélène without giving any technical details that she had a malignant brain tumour. She looked crestfallen. She then asked a question I wasn't expecting from her:

"Am I going to die?"

There was a brief pause during which I was panicking – 'what's he going to say? Surely he's not going to say, 'yes, you're going to die." But, I needn't have worried, Mr Mendoza was the consummate professional. He said gently and simply:

"We're all going to die."

This was code for: 'I am not going to lie to you, but there's no need to ask these questions if you don't want to know.'

Marie-Hélène didn't want to know, so the conversation changed to treatment options. The biopsy was scheduled for the following Thursday and then in a few weeks radiotherapy would commence:

"You will be treated by Dr Mark Glaser," said Mr Mendoza, "He gets excellent results – he's like a one-man army."

*****

Marie-Hélène remained in hospital for three weeks. During that time, her sister Béatrice, and her mother were staying with me in Banberry. I did not find it easy. I had always struggled to get on with Marie-Hélène's mother, and having her at close quarters did not improve our relationship. It was all reasonably polite and civilised, but I was frustrated by the fact that Marie-Hélène's family had a completely different approach to her illness. They told me off when they overheard me telling a concerned neighbour about Marie-Hélène's cancer. For them, it was a private, family matter and there was no need for people outside their immediate circle to know. However, they did not consider that I needed to find a way to cope too, and my way of coping was to be open about it without giving too much away. I was in shock at what had happened and at work was withdrawn. It was important to carry on as normal, but the new 'normal' was very different to the old 'normal'.

I was feeling increasingly isolated and the burden of knowledge about Marie-Hélène's illness weighed heavily on me. The person I would have liked to have talked to most was Marie-Hélène, but she was coping with it in her own way, and my duty was to support her. Supporting her meant respecting the fact that she did not want to hear anything negative or even contemplate the possibility that she might die. But Marie-Hélène also wanted her immediate family around her, so although her mother headed back to France after three weeks, her sister Béatrice remained with us for three years!

There were emotional times when Marie-Hélène did despair a little, but we went to a priest and she received unction (the sacrament of healing), which involved prayers and anointing her with oil. This gave Marie-Hélène strength. Another low point was when she saw a female consultant who was unfamiliar with Marie-Hélène and her approach to the brain cancer. Marie-Hélène talked about getting better and being determined to beat her illness. The consultant, wide-eyed, and thinking her a fantasist said:

"Do you know what the chances of beating this are?"

It was the complete opposite of what Marie-Hélène wanted to hear and she dissolved into tears. I was furious with the consultant for being that insensitive, and we ended the consultation almost immediately. Marie-Hélène was distraught so we went to the hospital chapel to pray quietly and to give her time to gather her strength.

Marie-Hélène did not start radiotherapy until the beginning of November. This gave us a chance to prepare for the fact that she was going to lose her hair. We investigated different places to buy wigs as the NHS wigs looked a little low quality to us! We wanted something that looked like a proper head of hair. Eventually, Marie-Hélène chose a very expensive and stylish blonde, shoulder length wig that looked remarkably life-like. I knew she had made the right choice when a couple of months later, a former colleague complimented her on her new hairstyle! When Marie-Hélène's hair did fall out, it fell out very quickly. I came back from school one day and half her hair had fallen out in the shower. By the next day, she was completely bald. I found it secretly a little distressing, but she took it in her stride, made jokes about it, and started wearing her wig.

Dr Glaser did indeed turn out to be the one-man army Mr Mendoza told us he was. Normally, someone with a brain tumour, would only have received a maximum of 60 grays radiotherapy. Because of her relatively young age, Marie-Hélène received 67 grays. This had to be done with pinpoint accuracy to avoid killing surrounding healthy, normal cells.

Radiotherapy as a treatment can only be given once, otherwise it will cause necrosis of brain cells. I was in awe of Dr Glaser's skills as a physician. He was a man on top of his game and had treated some notable people, including Mo Mowlam, a former Secretary of State for Northern Ireland.

Whilst Marie-Hélène was being treated, she was given steroids. This gave her a rapacious appetite; she regularly consumed two lunches and two dinners. She put on three stone in three months, and it was good to see her enjoying her food. I did not expect her to live very long so was determined that the more enjoyable I could make her life, the better. Her sister Béatrice similarly wanted to make her life fun, and we never missed an opportunity to laugh at life and the bizarre hand we had been dealt.

In February 1999, after Marie-Hélène had finished her treatment, we decided to go to Lourdes in the South of France in order to try the healing waters of the River Gave de Pau. It was a difficult trip as Marie-Hélène had been taken off her steroids and was recovering from radiotherapy. Physically, she was weak and could hardly eat. Whilst I tucked into three course meals, she would struggle to finish a bowl of soup. She lost almost all the weight she had put on.

Lourdes first gained notoriety in 1858 when a fourteen-year-old girl called Bernadette Soubirous allegedly had visions of the 'Immaculate Conception' (assumed to be Mary, mother of Jesus). The visions took place at a cave on the banks of the River Gave de Pau. After the Roman Catholic Church declared her visions to be genuine, a basilica was built above the cave (or 'grotte' as it is called in French). Lourdes became a place of pilgrimage and healing. Millions of people per year visit Lourdes in order to find spiritual or physical healing and there are 7000 documented cures associated with these visits. The Roman Catholic Church has only validated 67 of them as being miracles.

It was quiet in Lourdes when Marie-Hélène and I visited it. However, we were able to visit the different places of worship and the 'grotte'. We put the healing waters of the river on to the parts of the body which we wanted cured. So Marie-Hélène bathed her head in the water and I washed my knee!

Three months after we returned from Lourdes, Marie-Hélène had an MRI scan. It revealed that her brain tumour had disappeared.

CHAPTER 10

SUPPORTING SOFIA

"You can't solve anyone else's life for them. But then, if you see someone struggling with a heavy load, isn't it forbidden to walk on without helping them?"

Naomi Alderman, Disobedience

At the beginning of the Spring term 2013, I arranged a mentoring session with Sofia. Although I was no longer her form tutor, I would see her for chats now and again. I would always arrange these when I was on duty in the house area, as this was a public place, and I did not want these sessions to be misconstrued. On this occasion, Sofia was very stressed about her health, and I felt sorry for her. Later on, the same day, I sent her a follow-up email:

"Hi Sofia, I enjoyed our chat today, but was really sorry to hear that you've been so stressed out by your health. Needless to say, I'm always available for a chat & you're very much in my thoughts and prayers. God bless, S"

Sofia was also under pressure because she had not done very well in her AS Levels and was going to retake them all in May. I was very conscious that with her health being an issue, she could do with as much support as she could find.

Sofia wanted that support and would often appear in my classroom at unexpected times. Occasionally, she would come and work in my classroom during her free periods. She would use my room as her base when she was on study leave and revising for examinations, and she would always pop in for a chat after she had done a History or Philosophy examination. I was relaxed about this although I did feel a little uncomfortable when, on a few occasions, I found her working in my classroom at 8am in the morning!

There were, of course, lighter moments, with me sharing jokes and memes with Sofia and her friend Lucy. Humour is always a good way of relieving stress. I also sent Sofia a funny ecard for her 18th birthday, which she found very amusing and showed it to her friends and another teacher.

One incident that I remember clearly is an Ethics lesson that I did on 'In vitro fertilisation' (IVF). We were discussing as a class whether IVF should be available on the National Health Service (NHS). I said that I was against IVF being available on the NHS and put forward two arguments to support my point of view. Firstly, I argued that not being able to have children is not life-threatening or physically painful, so the finite resources of the NHS would be better spent elsewhere. Secondly, I argued that the world was already overpopulated, so we should not be spending money on helping people overpopulate the planet even more.

Normally, Sofia was quiet during lessons and did not say much, however, during my IVF lesson, she came alive. She challenged my point of view vigorously, and I was pleased – I always encouraged my students to argue with me and put forward different views.

After the lesson was over, I reflected on what Sofia had said, and then the penny dropped – Sofia was an IVF child! I already knew that her parents had met as teenagers and had been trying for a child for many years. Sofia had also told me that she had been one of twins, and twins are more common in IVF pregnancies as usually more than one embryo is implanted. Mrs Messina had told me that Sofia had been a miracle, but, on reflection, perhaps medical science had been the miracle worker, not St Agatha!

It was 12.30pm and I knew where Sofia would be, so I rushed outside and found her in the quad:

"You're an IVF child yourself aren't you," I said.

"I don't want anyone else to know but, yes, I am," replied Sofia.

"Look, I'm really sorry about what I said. I should have thought it through better…"

"It's alright," she said "Everyone is allowed their point of view."

Sofia was being remarkably gracious considering that I had just taught a lesson in which I had effectively implied that it would have been better if she had not been born! But that's not what I thought or wanted to imply! I had dropped a clanger, and it reminded me of one of the dangers of teaching controversial issues – you never know who has been personally affected by what you're talking about, so you should err on the side of caution. I had not.

I reflected on my views with regards to IVF and tried to work out why I had expressed such negativity towards it. One reason was because I am childless myself, and thought of myself as happily childless, but some people are not like that – they have a profound desire to have their own children and are deeply psychologically affected by an inability to reproduce. May be, I was one of those people myself and was unconsciously troubled by my childless state. Perhaps I was overcompensating by taking a hard line on IVF, a bit like a repressed homosexual exhibiting homophobic attitudes. I hastily put together an apology which I emailed to Sofia:

"Hi Sofia, I think that some of what I said in today's lesson may have been wrong and perhaps clouded by things in my own past. I need to rethink my views. Sorry about that. Regards, S"

I had never before hinted at my own vulnerabilities to a student, and fortunately Sofia never asked me what those things in my own past were. I was also at the time going through some very difficult personal circumstances dealing with family illness, but I did not want to burden Sofia with this either.

As time progressed that spring, my students made more and more demands on me for sample answers and individual help. Sofia and Lucy regularly turned up to lunchtime 'surgeries', and Lucy, in particular, would email me about subtle points of philosophical understanding, so that she could master the content of the examination specification. I was working flat out, doing my best for my students, and at the same time trying to cope with difficulties in my private life. It was taking a toll on me, and it was a relief when my A-Level candidates finally went on study leave in May.

However, some of them, realising they had not done enough work, were still pestering me for more help.

By this stage, Sofia was repeating all her AS examinations, and on the odd occasion when I saw her, she was appearing more and more tired. When she finished this first lot of exams, I sent her an email trying to give her some encouragement before her last set of A-Levels.

"Hi Sofia, Congratulations on getting through your AS exams. As they say in football parlance – it's a game of two halves! Hope you manage to renew your energy during half-term. Still rooting for you! S"

She replied simply, "Thanks :)"

At the beginning of June, Lucy and Sofia came to see me about an examination topic. Sofia revealed that she had been given a prize which she would receive on prize-giving day in July. Sofia asked me whether I would be attending prize-giving and I said that I would have to be at the church .service in the morning, and at lunchtime, but normally skipped the prize-giving itself. Quite a few staff did this, as it took place in a marquee that was stiflingly and unpleasantly hot and nobody kept a record of who managed to survive until the end of the ceremony! I told her that this year, seeing as she was getting a prize, I might attend it after all.

When it came to prize-giving day, Sofia came and sought me out in the morning for a chat. I was surprised that she had not turned up with either of her parents:

"My father's busy and my mother's recovering from her operation," said Sofia. I had not realised her mother had been in hospital, and I did not enquire as to the nature of her surgery. It seemed to me that I was in loco parentis for the day, so I had a chat with her before prize-giving in the afternoon, sat through the swelteringly hot ceremony in my suit, gown and hood, and said my goodbye to Sofia and her friends before going off to the pub with a mate.

Two days later, Sofia came into school to give 'thank you' gifts to her various teachers. She gave me a lovely bottle of Armagnac. Her mother was with her so it was a good opportunity to say goodbye to her. I had a quick chat with both of them and hugged them goodbye. Sofia asked me whether I would be at the leavers' barbecue that evening. I told her I would not be. I tended to avoid optional school social events such as barbecues and school promenades, as I would rather have been at home relaxing. In my absence, Sofia and Lucy went up to my classroom and wrote various amusing phrases on my white board, recalling funny things I had said and done. Their graffiti had been wiped off by a cleaner the next morning, but Sofia sent me a photo of what they had done. I was touched that they had made the effort.

I was pleased that Sofia left Farlbridge School so happy and it had been a privilege to support her as best as I could. I am acutely aware of the privilege and responsibility involved in being a teacher. However, with hindsight I realise now that I had allowed Sofia to become too dependent on me and at an unconscious level I had become dependent on her. There was something going on psychologically between us, and it bothered me. 'What is it about Sofia?' I thought to myself.

I assumed that once she had left school, that would be the end of my relationship with Sofia. However, after she left, we remained in contact for a while, which, it turned out, was not a good thing for either of us, as I was losing the plot.

CHAPTER 11

REMISSION

"A good half of the art of living is resilience."
Alain de Botton

After her initial treatment in the UK, Marie-Hélène chose to have her follow-up MRI scans done in France. So every few months we would go over to Lille for a scan, and then again a week later for the results. At first it was a bit like waiting for your GCSE, 'A' Level and degree results all rolled into one. Is it going to be good news or bad news?

Dr Dubois, Marie-Hélène's oncologist was, like us, delighted when he saw that there was no sign of her brain tumour. Marie-Hélène refused to look at the scans, but I was fascinated both by the technology and what they indicated about Marie-Hélène's health. Of course, we knew that just because the tumour had disappeared, that did not mean that Marie-Hélène was cured. It was more than likely that some cancerous cells remained.

In spring 1999, we decided to get a dog. We had read that dogs helped people rehabilitate after illness and that they were generally good for one's health. So, we bought a male Golden Retriever, called 'Scott'. Scott was the last dog left in the litter and being fairly ignorant about dogs, we did not notice that he had a leg deformity. It made him walk low down on his haunches. As a puppy, I used to have comments about this hurled at me when I was walking him, and was once stopped by the Police when they spotted it. People obviously thought we were mistreating him, but nothing could have been further from the truth. We doted on him. After six months, we took him to see a specialist, he was treated with a course of tablets made from shark cartilage, and his condition improved. We also tried hydrotherapy, but Scott hated water and could not swim. We only did one session of hydrotherapy as it seemed to traumatise him. We could not bear to put him through it again.

The other thing that Scott could not do, was retrieve. I would throw a ball, he would run after it, and then chew it. As hard as I tried to get him to bring the ball back, he just would not do it. It was strange having a Retriever that would not retrieve, but he had a very sweet, gentle, nature except when it came to squirrels which he would chase incessantly. But even with them, he lacked the killer instinct. Once, a young squirrel fell out of a tree in front of him, he grabbed it, looked surprised at having caught one at last, and then let it go. It scrambled back up the tree.

He was not aggressive to other dogs and did not bark, except when you had left him outside in the garden and he wanted to come back inside. As a guard dog, he was useless, trusting every person that came anywhere near the house. He would rather have licked someone to death than bite them. The only time we ever had problems with him was when there was a bitch in season anywhere within a half-mile radius. He was such a placid dog, that we did not feel the need to get him neutered. But his natural instincts kicked in when he smelt any dog in her heat cycle.

In the summer of 1999, we persuaded our dog breeders to look after Scott for a few weeks while we went on a camping tour of France. Marie-Hélène had fully recovered from her treatment and was in remission. However, we did not know what the future held and I was fearful that her brain cancer could come back at any time. The prognosis I had been given for her was so dire, I was mentally adjusting to losing her. I was expecting her to die within two years so I was determined that we were going to have fun together while we still could. My mindset about our future had changed so completely that my greatest fear was not her being dead. My biggest fear was observing her decline and seeing her in pain, and all the anguish and anxiety associated with that. There is nothing more psychologically painful than watching a loved one suffer.

Marie-Hélène and I had been camping together before. In 1995, we went to the West Coast of France, and for our honeymoon in 1996 we spent three weeks in the Côte d'Azur near Cannes in South East France. The following year we had camped in South West France near Béziers.

Camping in France during the summer is huge. Not only do hoards of French people explore their own country, but the campsites we visited always contained a high proportion of other Europeans. The Dutch Germans, Belgium and British are the nationalities most represented out of these. I have always marvelled in particular at the large number of people from The Netherlands that travel during the summer. So many, in fact, that it makes me wonder if anyone is left in Holland during August!

We bought a new tent for our 1999 grand tour of France, packed our 'M' registration Nissan Micra with our camping equipment and just went without pre-booking anything. We always camped in relative comfort taking with us two tents (a big one and a small one for emergencies), demountable shelving, two tables, fold up chairs, a washing up bowl, two jerry cans, cutlery, crockery, saucepans, a gas stove and gas canister, a small refrigerator, 50 metres of cable, a fan, light fittings, spare bulbs, blow up beds, duvets, sheets and pillows. In addition, we took clothing and a basic amount of water and food. It is amazing how much you can fit into a Nissan Micra!

Our first campsite was in central France at Saint-Gaultier on the banks of the River Creuse. It provided an opportunity for us to visit a couple of the lakes in the area and befriend our camping 'neighbours'. I remember one particular evening when we were invited over to their tent to partake of home distilled 'eau de vie'. There is a long tradition in France of making your own strong spirit from various fruits including plums and pears. These tend to be significantly stronger than your average bottle of whisky. I'm not an expert, but on this occasion, I enjoyed the taste of our new-found friends' eau de vie, and accepted a second, third, and then fourth glass. Marie-Hélène stopped after one. By the end of the evening, I loved my neighbours, and might even have told them so!

After Saint-Gaultier we went down to the Dordogne and stayed south of Sarlat-la-Canéda on the banks of the river.

It is an incredibly beautiful area of France with the river Dordogne surrounded by steep tree-lined banks and rocky outcrops. Sarlat, itself, is a charming medieval town.

From the Dordogne we headed down to Lourdes once again for further spiritual sustenance. It was the height of the season and I was touched by the sight of ill and dying people on pilgrimage, being pushed in special wheelchairs by their helpers. In the evening, a candlelit procession of pilgrims takes place with singing and prayers. Whatever one's beliefs or non-beliefs, it is difficult not to be moved by the experience.

We headed up the West Coast after leaving Lourdes. I almost drowned in Biarritz after being hit on the head by a surfer. The sea is notoriously dangerous there and is constantly surveyed. Semi-conscious, the waves rolled me over and over again, dragging me under, until I managed to regain my faculties and strength to swim back to shore. As I staggered back up the beach spluttering and gasping for air, I walked past four life guards who evidently hadn't seen a thing. They did not even enquire if I was alright.

Our last campsite was on Isle d'Oléron, which is the largest island on the West Coast of France. Our favourite place there was the fishing port of La Cotinière, where we ate the best fresh prawns we had ever had.

Our summer holiday of 1999 stands out as the happiest time Marie-Hélène and I ever spent together. After all that we had been through together over the previous year, it was an opportunity just to be together and relax, and thank God that we were still standing, still laughing, and still enjoying life.

*****

After Marie-Hélène was diagnosed with brain cancer, she never worked again. But she had a new job, and that job was survival. Her focus was looking after herself and keeping as healthy as possible. Every day she would drink freshly squeezed orange juice and take selenium tablets which she found out were good for the brain. She took a small dose of Sodium Valproate, which is an anti-epilepsy drug, and drank only a minimal amount of alcohol. She would walk Scott as much as she could and made sure that she did not put on too much weight.

Marie-Hélène was also spending an increasing amount of time in France and having regular MRI scans, which showed that she continued to be cancer-free.

I occupied myself by developing my career, getting involved in local politics, being a school governor, and expanding my circle of friends. In 2000, I left Banberry Grammar School after six years, and became Director of Studies at St Patrick's School in Barnbridge, Surrey. It was a promotion that meant I was spending less time in the classroom and more time doing curriculum management, timetabling and strategic planning. However, in terms of teaching, I did develop a new string to my bow when I started teaching A Level Philosophy. It was a new challenge that I relished. I struck up a friendship with the then Headmistress, Margaret Jackson, and came to understand the demands and rewards of being a senior manager.

Between 1999 and 2002, Marie-Hélène and I grew apart as my career blossomed and her focus was on her health. At one point I had a brief affair with a woman unconnected with work. It is not something I am proud of as I behaved badly, but when the physical side of a marriage dies, it is not uncommon for people to stray.

For me, Marie-Hélène's stable health was a relief, but it also meant I had to change my mindset. I had been told that she was going to die within a short period of time, and had mentally prepared for that. Yet, it seemed there was a possibility that she might live for another ten or twenty years, or even more. I had to adjust to the possibility that she might live.

With the prospect that we might have a long-term future together, there was only one question that mattered to me: What are we going to do? She had four major interests: Her health, her family, me and our dog, Scott. I shared three of these interests but I struggled with her family. They were good people but her mother had such a different approach to life, that I was feeling increasingly alienated from her. Whereas I came from a liberal background in which, for instance, women priests and gay marriage seemed inevitable and sensible social developments, Marie-Hélène and most of her family found such ideas anathema. Whereas I approached Marie-Hélène's illness by wanting to be open about it, her family did not want to face the reality of it. And when I tried to start a debate or argue about these differences, I was met with intransigence. There was not even the possibility of having the sort of debate at the end of which you agree to disagree, and respect each other for being able to put forward your point of view cogently.

As for my interests, Marie-Hélène shared few of them. She wasn't interested in my family, in my friends or my job. In my first term at St Patrick's School we were invited to dinner by Margaret Jackson. The Deputy Head and her husband were also there. Marie-Hélène was so rude to everyone that I left in a state of acute embarrassment. Margaret later told me that everyone had felt sorry for me! Looking back, Marie-Hélène was more sociable before she got ill, but she was never someone who could be bothered to feign interest in people who she did not like. The French have a reputation for being rude, and although I am wary of generalisations based on culture or nationality, in this respect Marie-Hélène conformed to the stereotype!

In August 2001, my father was diagnosed with leukaemia. This did little to help my relationship with Marie-Hélène as I now had another difficulty with which to deal that took the focus away from her. At first, my father was told that his type of leukaemia would develop slowly and that he would not need treatment straight away. However, he became ill quickly and by November, he had been admitted to hospital and put on chemotherapy.

By spring 2002, I was so concerned about the state of my relationship with Marie-Hélène that I persuaded her to attend marriage counselling sessions with me. I found the first session helpful but Marie-Hélène was not happy about it. The counsellor suggested we needed eight more sessions but Marie-Hélène said simply:

"If we have those sessions we'll end up divorced." I found this statement both reassuring and troubling. On the one hand she was acknowledging that there were problems in our marriage. On the other hand, she was indicating that she was not prepared to address those problems. I was not going to force her to attend sessions with which she was not going to engage. So that was the end of our marriage counselling.

Our relationship improved when we went on a camping holiday to the Ardèche in the summer of 2002, but in the autumn, Marie-Hélène was spending more and more time in France. Things were at breaking point, and I was considering throwing in the towel when Marie-Hélène rang me in early December. She had some news for me: her most recent scan had shown a change in her condition. Her brain tumour was back.

CHAPTER 12

LOSING THE PLOT

"It is better to lock up your heart with a merciless padlock, than to fall in love with someone who doesn't know what they mean to you."

Michael Bassey Johnson, The Infinity Sign

In June 2013, Sofia sent me a friendship request on Facebook which I accepted. I was happy to accept friendship requests from former pupils and had done so from other students as well. Our Facebook relationship was quite normal with each of us liking our respective posts. On one occasion I was on holiday in Italy with my wife when I posted a picture of myself. Within seconds Sofia had liked it. I was flattered so, when she posted something sweet on line, I liked it and made a short comment.

In August, I decided to contact her directly. It was coming up to A-Level results day, and I wanted to touch base with her beforehand. We exchanged a few friendly and funny messages, some of which related to the very different summers we were having. Whereas I was having a very quiet time in South London after I had returned from holiday, Sofia had gone to Sicily and was doing her duty visiting what seemed like an endless stream of relatives:

"I've seen about seventy people in the last two weeks," she wrote just before she returned to the UK to get her results.

"I've seen about seven," I replied, "and most of those I haven't talked to!"

On results day, I got up early to check out how my students had done in their exams. The Lower Sixth results in both History and Philosophy were excellent going beyond my expectations, but the Philosophy results for Sofia's year were disastrous. I looked unbelievingly at how badly they had done. Lucy, whom I had predicted an A*, had done particularly poorly, with an 'E' in her Philosophy of Mind paper and a 'U' in her Ethics paper. Sofia had also missed out on the grade I had predicted her, however her other subjects had come to the rescue, and she had got what she needed to get into her first-choice university.

It was the worst set of A-Level results that I had experienced in twenty-five years of teaching. Something had gone badly wrong and I knew what it was – the marking. I had long since lost faith in the examination system. The quality of marking varied tremendously and there was a subjectivity that made it almost impossible to make accurate predictions about students' potential achievement. I would sometimes predict A*'s and students achieved B's. Other times, it worked the other way round. Normally, the marking in one paper would be overgenerous which would balance out the overharsh marking in another paper. Consequently, students achieved roughly what they deserved. However, in the summer of 2013, both papers had been marked by people who obviously did not have a clue what they were doing and we ended up with the disaster scenario I had feared would eventually befall a cohort of students.

It took three months of appeals and remarks to sort the mess out, by which time almost all students had their final grade improved, but I still felt the results did not properly reflect the quality of their writing.

As a head of department, I was required to be in school for results day, but this time I was dreading it. What was I going to say to my disappointed students and parents? I need not have worried as everyone was surprisingly understanding about it. When I arrived, Sofia was there with other members of her year group. I exchanged a few words with her and some other students and parents, and then retreated to my office. I had arranged to meet Lucy and her mother there. However, it was Sofia that turned up with Lucy, so I stood at the door of my office and had a brief conversation with them. Sofia was in good form as she had got her grades, Lucy was in fighting mood, affronted at the examination board for getting it wrong, and I was just feeling terrible at what had happened. They seemed surprised that I was taking it so personally. However, I could not help but feel a failure, even though I knew that I should have, as Rudyard Kipling urged, met 'with triumph and disaster, and treat those two imposters just the same.'

Afterwards, I felt bad that I had been so downbeat and not happier for Sofia, so I sent her a message congratulating her on her success and offering to take her and Lucy out for lunch to celebrate their respective successes. She replied with a 'thumbs up' emoji. Neither Sofia nor Lucy ever got back to me about it, so our celebration lunch never happened.

When I got back to work at the beginning of September I was at a low ebb. Despite excellent AS Level Philosophy results and very good History grades, all I could think about was the terrible results that had befallen Sofia's year group. More than that, I felt an emptiness inside because she was no longer there. Sofia had been an ever-present part of my professional life for years, and a reassuring presence at that. Now I was alone. It felt like a bereavement. May be that partly explains what happened next:

I woke on Tuesday 10th September in what I can only describe as a state of 'love-sickness'. And when I say this, I am not exaggerating. For the first time in my life, I felt physically sick because of romantic feelings – my stomach was in knots and I wanted to puke. Perhaps it was worse because I knew it was an impossible love, and consciously, I knew it was a disaster. But there was no denying it, my feelings for Sofia were so strong that I could not think of anything or anyone else. It was pathetic that I had suddenly switched from being very fond of Sofia to being madly in love with her. It was weird and frightening, and I could not explain it. I did not even realise that it was possible as I had never experienced anything like it before. 'This is a fucking disaster,' I thought to myself, 'have you gone mad?' I had, and in my madness, I started having a fantasy that perhaps I could make it work between Sofia and me, even though it would have meant abandoning my wife.

That evening I contacted Sofia. I couldn't tell her that I had fallen in love with her and had a fantasy about running away with her, so I wrote her a friendly message saying that it wasn't the same at school without her. She responded, and that evening we exchanged a few messages talking about the debacle that had been that year's Philosophy A-Level results.

My life was spiralling out of control at a mental level – I had fallen in love with an eighteen-year-old girl who was more than young enough to be my daughter. I had to get a grip.

I tried to act normal and professional, so, when I found out that her A Level remark had been successful and she had gone up a grade, I sent her a formal message, and wished her well for her upcoming studies at university. I was trying to draw a line under our relationship and give her the space to move on. My romantic feelings towards her were so strong that I knew I was no longer any use to her.

By the beginning of October, I decided that there was only one course of action that made sense. I would have to cut Sofia out of my life altogether, so I blocked her on Facebook.

Blocking her was a relief, as it gave me greater control of my emotions and I reasoned that sometimes you have to be cruel to be kind. I knew that it would upset her. It was not easy weaning myself of my Sofia obsession, but when one has an addiction, 'cold turkey' is often the right way to go. In hindsight, I should have sought therapy, as that would have supported me at a time in my life when I felt particularly vulnerable. But I did not.

Things started to improve a little over the next couple of months, and I made a huge mental effort to try to forget

Sofia. However, I was like a non-drinking alcoholic with whom it would only take one drink, and they would be back on the bottle with a vengeance.

That 'one drink' happened at the end of term. We were due to break up on Wednesday 18th December. On the Monday, six former History students from Sofia's year group popped into see me during a lesson that some sixth formers had decided would become a party to celebrate Christmas and one of their birthdays. I was touched that my former students wanted to see me, and we took a couple of selfies, which I sent to them by creating a Facebook group called 'Former History Crew'.

I was relieved that Sofia was not amongst the students who had surprised me on that Monday. It would not have helped cure me of my obsession if she had turned up. However, it only took one more day before I heard from her via her mother.

On Tuesday afternoon, I received two messages from Mrs Messina. The first one said that Sofia had enjoyed her first term at university, had made a good circle of friends, and had improved in confidence. The seconds one said that Sofia would pop in to see me in the New Year. I imagined Sofia standing next to her mother, telling her what to write. It felt like her way of getting back in touch with me even though I had blocked her on Facebook. I replied to Mrs Messina by saying that I was delighted Sofia had had a good first term, and that I had missed her, and would be pleased if she came to see me.

I was in turmoil. All my efforts at trying to cure myself of my Sofia-addiction had failed, so I resolved to lay all my cards on the table, and see what happened. Like a desperate poker player, I was going for 'win or bust'. In reality, of course, it was a 'lose, lose' scenario however she reacted, but I was in the throes of a mental breakdown and my sanity had deserted me. So I sent Sofia a friendship request on Facebook, which she accepted, and then, after testing the water with one communication, sent her the message that would change my life forever.

It is a bizarre, looking back, to think that someone with my level of experience, who had a well-paid job, would risk everything in such a kamikaze way. I was going against everything I knew to be true and had become utterly self-obsessed, as well as obsessed with Sofia. I had become the cliché of the older man in a mid-life crisis chasing after the younger woman. But there was something else going on that I was struggling to understand. I knew deep down that I needed help, that my actions were a cry for help. That help came two days later from an unlikely source – Sofia's mother: Mrs Francesca Messina.

CHAPTER 13

SURGERY

"Surgeons can cut out everything except cause."
Herbert M Shelton

It was a shock when Marie-Hélène told me that her tumour had regrown. She had been in remission for four years and all the MRI scans up to that point had shown an absence of cancer. I had got so used to her having regular scans, that they had begun to barely register on my calendar. I had not accompanied her to Lille for either the scan or the follow-up as I had been working. I had become blasé, almost complacent about her health. But, now, we had to go back into 'action' mode and decide what to do next. Consequently, we sought advice both in England and France.

I was keen on her being treated in the United Kingdom, so I telephoned Marie-Hélène's former consultant from Charing Cross hospital, Nigel Mendoza, and asked what he would recommend. After expressing surprise that she was still alive, he said that surgery was a possibility, but risky. His suggestion was to try chemotherapy first, and once again steered us in the direction of the one-man-army; Dr Mark Glaser.

Marie-Hélène and I went to see Dr Glaser for a consultation in early January 2003. He was marvellous – straightforward, upbeat without being unrealistic, and warm. At the end of the consultation he hugged Marie-Hélène, which touched me. It was great to see someone of his stature being able to dispense with formalities and show spontaneous human affection.

In the end, Marie-Hélène opted for being treated in France. It was her choice, and although it was not my favoured option, I did not put any pressure on her. Once she made the decision, I supported her totally.

When we went to see her surgeon in Lille, he explained that he was going to take out the right frontal lobe of her brain, which the tumour had invaded. He seemed confident that the operation would be a success, although he did say that there was a ten percent chance that she would not survive. This seemed high to me, but not as bad as if you were the first person to use the gun in a game of Russian roulette. The surgery appeared to be a bit of a roll of the dice, even if there was, in reality, little else in terms of options. The operation was scheduled for February 2003.

I was a little horrified that Marie-Hélène required a lobotomy so researched what effect this might have on her. I found out that removing the right frontal lobe could result in people having less ambition, poor concentration and becoming less inhibited. I did not relish the prospect of her personality changing, but as this was the course of action recommended to us, we decided the best thing was to just get on with it.

The evening before her operation, I took Marie-Hélène to the Centre Hospitalier Régional Universitaire de Lille (CHRU). I was very nervous, but for Marie-Hélène it was unimaginably more difficult. There was no getting away from it – this was major surgery with significant risks, and I could not help wondering whether this could be our last evening together. We had gathered together a series of prayers based on keeping people safe in times of trouble. We read these prayers together and then I held her hand as I prayed for her safe recovery from surgery. It was highly emotional and I left her with a heavy heart, once again in awe of her courage. Her surgery was scheduled for 9am the next day, so I promised I would come in early in the morning to see her before she was wheeled off to theatre.

The next morning, I got up early and drove the 40 miles from her family's house to Lille, so that I was able to spend a few moments with her before she went into theatre. She was nervous but positive, and was very much in a 'let's get this done' frame of mind. Marie-Hélène was then taken for surgery, and I went back to Bruay to begin the waiting game.

The hospital had told me that they would telephone me once she was conscious after the operation. They warned me that this may take some time, so I was not expecting to hear from them until late afternoon.

There was a lot of pacing around and biting of finger nails that day. Marie-Hélène's family was just as nervous as me. We didn't talk much about it, but each of us got on with our own thing holding our own private thoughts. I took Scott for a walk, we had lunch, although nobody was particularly hungry, and Marie-Hélène's mother prayed using her rosary.

Late afternoon came and went, but no news from the hospital. Evening arrived and still no news. Eventually, at 8pm the phone rang. It was not good. Marie-Hélène was still unconscious, she was fitting, and they were having trouble stabilising her. 'Fuck!' I thought.

There seemed to be a real possibility that Marie-Hélène would not pull through, so that night, nobody slept particularly well. I did, somehow, manage six hours sleep, but about three hours was the average for the rest of the family.

The phone rang at about 7.30am the next morning. A nurse talked to me in a grave voice, explaining that Marie-Hélène had been taken into surgery for a second time during the night in order to deal with a haematoma (bleeding) on the brain. She said they weren't sure she was going to survive and that I had better come to the hospital straightaway.

I was devastated and started to cry. Marie-Hélène's mother was not very sympathetic so I retreated to my car and bawled my eyes out there. Once I had pulled myself together, I rang my family, explained the situation and said that I wanted some support. Once again, I felt isolated and lonely in the face of a situation nobody seemed to be able to deal with.

I got to the hospital with Marie-Hélène's eldest sister Collette just after 9am. I walked into the neurosurgery department expecting to hear the worst. Instead I encountered Marie-Hélène's surgeon with a broad smile on his face:

"C'est loin d'être catostrophique!" he exclaimed [It's far from being a catastrophe].

He put up the post-operative scan which showed that he had done a very neat surgical job. As usual, I was fascinated by the scan; how it showed almost a perfect straight line where the right frontal lobe had been removed. He explained that he had taken out all of the tumour, and that they had put a drain in Marie-Hélène's head to release the pressure caused by the haematoma. This was not a cure, but he was confident that she would make a full recovery from surgery once she had come round from the induced coma in which they had put her.

I was surprised by how upbeat he was being when the telephone call I had received at 7.30am had been so negative. I raised this with him and he speculated that the person making the call had probably not had all the information to hand.

Although it was not visiting hours, I was allowed to see Marie-Hélène. She was in the intensive care ward of the neurology department. Her surgeon warned me that she would have tubes down her throat and nose, and that she was on a respirator. I was moved when I saw her all wired up, and a drain that went into her skull. Once again, I marvelled at the technology and asked questions about what various wires and tubes were for. I found it reassuring to know that the hospital was giving her the best possible care and this helped me cope with seeing her in such a poorly state. I stroked her hand and told her I loved her. There was no response – she was in a deep coma.

Later that day my mother and sister Elizabeth arrived. I felt a little embarrassed that I had brought them over when the situation was not as bad as I had initially thought. However, they did not seem to mind, and were treating the whole thing as a weekend excursion, albeit an emotionally demanding one. They had booked accommodation, so once they had seen Marie-Hélène in the afternoon, they were able to go back to their Campanile Hotel for dinner. I joined them, glad to have some support from my family. They were both on good form and cheered me up. I had been abstaining from alcohol for three months, but my mother poured me a large glass of red wine and said, "Drink up – you need this." She was right – the wine relaxed me.

Two days later the medical team took Marie-Hélène off the drug that had put her in an induced coma. They had assured me that she would come round quickly. However, that proved not to be the case – a day became two days and Marie-Hélène was still in a coma. Two days became three, four, five days, and then a week. Marie-Hélène was still in a coma. By this stage, I was becoming anxious, but as she began her second week in a coma, there were signs that she was responding a little. After two weeks, she was completely conscious and started talking. She was transferred to a normal ward.

I returned to work briefly, but when I did, I got word that my father had been rushed into hospital. It was a Friday, so I went to see him during my lunch break, as the Surrey hospital he was admitted to, was only a twenty-five-minutes' drive from my place of work. He was neutropenic which meant his immune system was severely compromised. I was not able to touch him or get near to him, but he seemed in remarkably good spirits. I went back to school, taught a lesson in the afternoon and then got back in my car to see Marie-Hélène in France. I bombed down the M20, got on the Channel Tunnel and then drove to the Lille hospital where Marie-Hélène was, arriving just before the end of visiting hours. Whilst lying in bed that night, I wondered whether anyone else that day had visited two close relatives in different hospitals, two hundred miles apart, in countries separated by a sea. It seemed to me that my life was becoming overwhelmed with family illness.

Marie-Hélène had been in bed for three weeks when she was told that she needed to get out of bed and walk. Her leg muscles were weak and she was apprehensive about getting back on her feet. However, the medical staff were very insistent – there was no reason why she could not walk, so walk she would.

I held her up by her shoulders as she tentatively took her first steps since the lobotomy. Her balance was not great, but she managed to make it from her bed, out of the room, and then down the corridor. I then helped her back to her room, and she sat down on her bed exhausted. We then gave her a Zimmer frame to use, and at first she was a little apprehensive, but within half an hour, she was able to get around on her own. She was weak, but mobile. The next day she was told to go home. The hospital needed her bed.

It took Marie-Hélène a couple of months to recover from her operation. She recuperated in France, and then eventually came back to our house in Banberry. I had, for a couple of years run the household, doing all the cooking and most of the housework. Marie-Hélène was now more dependent on others than ever, although she did regain the ability to walk.

The operation had indeed had an impact on her personality. She had become more childlike and sweet, laughing at silly things. She was more placid, rarely getting angry about anything. She had lost the will to do anything substantial apart from basic tasks. I remember being frustrated when I came back from school one day, and she was still in her pyjamas. I asked her what she had done all day. Her reply was:

"I've done two things today – I got up and I made myself some breakfast."

It was not that she was depressed; it was simply that her lobotomy had deprived her of the motivation to do virtually anything apart from survive.

Her sister had moved out of the house in 2001 and was now living with my friend Paul. However, she used to pop in and help out when she could. I was grateful when they joined us on our 2003 summer camping holiday, as it meant I had help looking after Marie-Hélène. Whilst we were on that holiday Marie-Hélène celebrated her 40th birthday. It was a major achievement given how much she had been through over the previous five years.

On the night of her 40th birthday, I lay down on my blow-up mattress and reflected on how much Marie-Hélène had changed since I first met her fifteen years earlier. I remembered how much initiative she had shown and how passionate she was in her twenties. I remembered how happy she had been on our wedding day, and how we had been hopeful that we would have our own family. But everything had been taken away from her by her illness, an illness I secretly and irrationally blamed myself for. I had read that pregnancy can trigger brain tumours to become more aggressive, and I remembered that a year before she was diagnosed, Marie-Hélène had had an early miscarriage. That was the beginning of it all. Her symptoms started six months after that. I had not given her a child, I had given her cancer.

CHAPTER 14

FALLOUT

"Words have consequences."
Albert Marrin

After sending my inappropriate message in December 2013, I sat in my car, outside the Co-op in Forest Hill, looking at our exchange of messages. Sofia had written:

"Your words are lovely but I don't understand why you blocked me?? I never expected that from someone like you 🙁"

I looked at her words again, and reckoned her confusion was that I had acted in a way that she was not expecting and had been cruel by blocking her. When I had re-friended her a couple of days earlier, I had looked at her Facebook posts for the period after I had blocked her. I was struck by how negative Sofia's posts had become after I cut her off. Her posts talked about heartache, and being let down, and so forth. The combination of this and her confused face reply, made me think that my blocking her had affected her deeply.

In that context, my response had made some sort of perverse sense:

"I know, it was cruel, but I was losing control of my emotions. It was my way of trying to get back some control in my life and giving you a chance to move on. But it didn't work because I just can't stop loving you Sofia. I should have trusted you more and told you how I felt. That's what I'm doing now… x"

I waited a few minutes, and there was no reply from Sofia. I tried looking at her Facebook page, and got a 'something has gone wrong' message. I went back to Messenger, and our conversation had disappeared. I realised that Sofia had now blocked me and that my message would go unanswered.

I went into the Co-op to do my shopping and thought, 'Well, that's the end of that.' I felt sad because I had loved Sofia, but also relieved that it was all over. She had done me a favour by blocking me, and I trusted her enough to think that she would not use the message I had sent against me.

*****

When Sofia's mother contacted me two days later, I was not entirely surprised. Sofia had understandably told her mother about my message. In fact, it was worse than that, because Sofia had taken a screenshot of it before blocking me. So, her mother had seen my message in black and white. She rang me whilst I was in the barber's. I hastily made my excuses and retreated to my car whilst I talked to Francesca Messina.

"Sofia has shown me a message that you sent her. Does this mean what I think it means?" said Mrs Messina

"This is difficult for me to talk about, as I haven't actually talked to anyone else about my feelings for Sofia, but, umm, yes, I do have those feelings. I basically woke up one day and thought 'I'm in love with Sofia – that's a disaster.'"

"But this won't do. I mean… you've got someone at home… Sofia must be twenty years younger than you… there's no way…."

"Yes, I realise that, but she is exceptional and I can't help the way I feel..."

"Look, why don't we meet up and talk this through – you obviously need some help… Are you one of those paedophiles?"

"No, I'm not like that."

"You know, Sofia's really upset. She's been shaking, crying, having difficulty breathing. I've been having heart palpatations – we're really shocked"

"Oh, I am sorry, I didn't intend it to have that effect."

"It's like you've taken her childhood away. She's afraid you're going to turn up at the door any minute. She said to me, "But Sir knows where we live.""

"No, I wouldn't do that – it's important to respect people's privacy"

"She doesn't feel safe… she wants to tell her father about it… but if he finds out… I wouldn't be able to help you… you know we could formally complain about you."

"Yes, I realise that."

"Look, I think we should meet, just the two of us... I know a pub round the corner where we could have a chat... and may be I can help you sort this all out."

"That's very kind of you – I really appreciate your compassion. Look, I'm really sorry about all this."

"But first of all, you need to send Sofia an apology through me."

"Okay I'll do that. What do you want me to say?"

"You need to say sorry for your message, and tell her you won't contact her again. She's also now frightened of men and doesn't trust them."

"And you want the apology sent to your phone, and you'll show it to Sofia?"

"Yes, to my phone. Please don't contact Sofia directly."

"I won't."

"You'll do that then."

"Yes, of course – I'll send the apology shortly."

"Thank you – goodbye."

"Okay, bye."

After I got off the phone, I felt terrible. I had not only freaked Sofia out, but her mother. And of course, I should have anticipated this reaction - of course she was going to panic. 'And now that I've been so irrational, she thinks I'm going to stalk her,' I thought. I knew that Sofia spent time by herself watching movies – 'she's probably imagining me as a male version of Glenn Close in the film, "Fatal

Attraction'", I wondered preposterously. 'Perhaps she thinks I'm going to boil her cat in a saucepan!'

One message was already having an impact way beyond what I intended. And it was only the beginning. I could not help thinking that I had been a fucking idiot. Yes, I had been a prize plonker! But worse than that, I had been utterly selfish, hurt Sofia and betrayed my wife.

I felt sorry for Mrs Messina, stuck in the middle between a father who was fiercely protective of his daughter and a distressed daughter. Francesca was trying her best to manage the situation without hurting me too much and I appreciated it. And then I started thinking the obvious question – why had I done it? Why had I scored such a ridiculous home goal? I must have completely lost my mind.

So, after I had finished in the barber's, I sat in my car and composed my apology to Sofia:

"Dear Sofia, your mother has asked me to send you this message via her phone. I am deeply sorry for expressing feelings towards you that I should not have had. Your mother tells me that you were shocked and traumatised, for which I am even more sorry. The message I sent you was as a result of personal difficulties I have been having which are not your fault and nothing to do with you. So, I am very sorry to have involved you. Please do not let my failure here make you disillusioned or mistrustful of others. You were right to block me on Facebook, and I won't contact you again. Once again, I apologise for the distress that I have caused you. I wish you all the very best for the future. Regards, Charles King"

I sent the apology as an imessage to Mrs Messina. She never received it. I don't know why she never got my apology though I think it was because of a technical fault that existed at the time with Apple phones and imessaging. Whatever the reason, the apology never arrived, and that made my situation even worse. I did not realise at the time that my apology had not been received, so assuming that she had seen it, I hoped that Sofia would now have greater peace of mind. 'Give it a few weeks, and this will all have blown over,' I thought to myself. I could not have been more wrong.

When I got home from the barber's, I reflected on the pickle I had got myself into and came to the conclusion that I had completely lost the plot. I thought about Mrs Messina offering to meet up with me to talk it all through and realised that she was right – I needed help. A cloud was lifting from my eyes as I started to realise how selfish and self-obsessed I had become. 'This cannot continue', I thought to myself – 'I need to get some therapy. I need to deal with my past otherwise I will be of no use to anyone.'

I googled 'counsellors' for the local area, and found a woman who advertised herself as an 'integrative counsellor'. Her name was Sandra Sutton, and I saw that she lived just a few hundred metres from me. So, I gave her a call.

Sandra was very professional. She asked a few basic questions, and I explained my past, and the various issues I needed to discuss with her. She told me that she was going away for Christmas, but would be back in early January. We arranged a counselling session for 3rd January 2014.

After I had made the phone call, I felt a huge weight lifting off my shoulders. I had made the first step towards healing, and that felt good. I also felt grateful to Mrs Messina for pointing me in the right direction. She did not - and probably still does not - realise how helpful her phone call was to me.

I went to see my wife and said to her:

"I don't think I've been myself recently and thought it might be useful if I got some counselling. What do you think?"

"Great idea – it's what you need – you're not easy to live with, so anything that helps you deal with your issues is good."

My wife had been there all along, knowing that I had lost my way, and waiting for me to see it for myself. The only thing, was that she had no idea just how far I had lost the plot mentally and emotionally. And I did not want to hurt her by telling her that I had fallen in love with a former student.

It was the 23rd December, and we were due to host my family for Christmas. I felt that we had turned a corner, and things could only get better from here. I knew that I had left myself vulnerable with the `message I had sent to Sofia, but I had now apologised, so hopefully we could move on.

CHAPTER 15

PARTING

"To say goodbye is to die a little."
Raymond Chandler, The Long Goodbye

By 2004, Marie-Hélène's health had stabilised. She was once again in remission, could walk short, but not long distances, and had settled into a tranquil existence of not doing a lot. She would, as usual, divide her time between France and England. When she was in England, and I was not working, I used to make sure she got up, got dressed and did some sort of task such as washing up or folding clothes. I found it depressing if she did not have some sort of disciplined routine. When she went to France, however, there was no pressure on her to do anything. She used to get up when she wanted, get dressed, or not get dressed, and was looked after very well by her family.

Once again our lives were diverging, and I was feeling increasingly isolated. Illness always brought us closer together, but remission presented more problems for me. Perhaps it was because I felt fine, had lots of energy, and was immersing myself in work, whereas Marie-Hélène was focused on only one thing – staying alive. We had very little in common anymore apart from our dog Scott. When there was a health crisis, it gave us something we could both focus on but when she was well, I found her irritating and was being nasty in the way I talked to her. This, in turn, made me feel guilty.

Of course, I should have been more patient, loving and understanding, but I was trying to hold down a full-time job as well as look after her. If we were going to stay together, I would need help, so I took Marie-Hélène to see her GP, who suggested getting a carer in. I was keen on this idea, but Marie-Hélène was having none of it. She wanted to be in France, or she wanted me looking after her. She did not want a stranger in our house. I then considered packing up my job and going to France to live with her there, but I was only thirty-eight, earning good money in the United Kingdom and had a mortgage to pay. Moreover, I enjoyed my work as Director of Studies at St Patrick's School. My job seemed to be the only thing that was preventing me from having a mental breakdown, so I was not going to give that up.

By the summer of 2004, I came to the conclusion that the only solution was for us to split up. Marie-Hélène would live permanently in France, where she really wanted to be, and I would live in the UK, which is where I wanted to be. The years of illness, of remission, of constantly going back and forth to the North of France had finally broken me and worn me down. I had had enough.

In July, my father's health took a turn for the worse, so I went over to see him in his home in Godalming. I was shocked by how bad Philip looked. He was only 72, but he looked so much older. He was pale, out of breath and very thin. He was dying of leukaemia.

My sister Elizabeth and I took him to hospital the next day to see his consultant. Over the previous three years he had undergone different forms of chemotherapy, but none had worked very well. His condition had responded to high doses of steroids but these were only a temporary help. The consultant was kind but honest. He told my father gently that they had run out of treatment options and that we had come to the end of the road. He said that they could put him back on large doses of steroids again, but he was sceptical about this, as he was not sure my father's weakened body would be able to cope with such powerful drugs.

My father bravely asked how long he had to live, and the doctor said, "Three months." This was longer than I had expected him to say, but my father looked crushed.

Elizabeth was also very upset to hear the consultant's prognosis, but rather than breaking down in front of us, she sensibly made an excuse for getting out of the situation. My father and I sat in the waiting room while they sorted out his admission to hospital. He was too ill to go back home. He started crying and I held his hand. I had not held my father's hand since I had been a child, but it seemed the right thing to do when he was facing the end of his life:

"It's not that I'm afraid of death," he sniffled, "it's just that I'm rather enjoying life and don't want to leave your mother."

"Have you had *the* conversation with her?" I asked.

"Yes, we've discussed my dying, and it's been difficult, but we've agreed that if she's not there when I pass away, it doesn't change anything. It's what we shared in life that's important."

I was deeply moved and impressed by my father's selfless love and courage. He was thinking of others rather than himself. I sat there feeling privileged to be able to spend that time with him. I never felt so close to him as I did at that moment, and still find it a source of inspiration.

My father opted to have large doses of steroids in an attempt to buy himself some more time. However, he was totally open about the fact that he was dying and even made jokes about it. One afternoon, he was discussing with us his funeral and what music, hymns and readings he would like. But then he suddenly came out with the following quip:

"You know the thing about dying is that millions of people have done it before, but nobody has ever complained!"

We laughed in the bitter-sweet way that humour in the face of tragedy elicits.

But it was not all laughs. One thing that was bothering my father was the memory of his sister Ronnie. My father was the eldest of three children. His younger brother Jim had died in 1997, but his sister had died in 1939 at the age of five (when Philip was seven). Jim had just been born so my father's parents had their hands full with two older children and a baby. That is possibly why they did not notice the van that ran over Ronnie outside their house early one morning. Philip had been playing chase with his younger sister, a game that in this case had ended in fatal consequences as she ran out on to the road and was killed.

My father was traumatised but his parents made him go to school the day that Ronnie was killed. Being in a state of shock, his trauma was exacerbated still further that very same day, when his teacher made him stand up in front of the whole class and recount what had happened. She then proceeded to use it as an example of why it was dangerous to play near a road. My father told me it took him fifty years to come to terms with these events.

Philip was the last person alive to be able to remember Ronnie, and he remembered his sister fondly. He would talk not just about her death but her red hair, her cheerful personality and sweet disposition. For him, keeping her memory alive had been important, and it bothered him that with his death, Ronnie would be forgotten. He said to my elder sister Pauline:

"Who's going to remember Ronnie when I've gone?"

"I'll remember Ronnie for you when you've gone," replied Pauline gently. And it is the same for me. Recounting the story of my father and his sister is a way of keeping alive Philip's memory of his beautiful red-headed sister, Ronnie, who died so tragically at the age of five.

Marie-Hélène was in France when my father was dying in hospital. Every day my mother, sisters and I would have precious time with Philip and were gradually saying goodbye. I wanted Marie-Hélène to be able to say her goodbye, because she had a relationship with him too. So I arranged to go over to France, and pick her up, so that she would be able to visit my father for at least one last time.

127

The day before I drove over to France to pick Marie-Hélène up, I went to Elizabeth's house to put some new felt on her shed roof. It was an awkward job, taking me a few hours. I then went over to see my father in hospital and met my godparents Patricia and Chris, who were visiting him. They had not seen him for a while and were shocked by how ill he looked. My father was in good form that day. The steroids had perked him up, he was walking, talking and joking as usual about life and death. It was one of the hottest days of the year, and I felt a sense of tranquillity as we sat and chatted amicably. After I left, Elizabeth, and her children arrived. My other sister Pauline also popped in.

The following day (Tuesday 3rd August), I went to France to pick up Marie-Hélène. When I arrived, I realised that I had left my mobile phone at home. It was lunchtime and Marie-Hélène was still not up. I tackled her mother about it saying that Marie-Hélène needed to be pushed to get up earlier and do something constructive. Eventually, Marie-Hélène appeared and we talked about my father. I explained what good form he had been in the previous day, but cautioned against too much optimism as the consultant had given him a prognosis of three months, and we were already two weeks into that. Marie-Hélène and I left Bruay in the afternoon, got stuck on the M25 and eventually arrived in Banberry after 7pm. When I got home, I found a text message from my mother on my phone, saying that Dad had taken a turn for the worse, and that she would be staying the night at the hospital.

I tried to ring my mother's mobile but there was no response. I rang my sister Elizabeth. Still no response. I rang Pauline and after a few rings, she answered the phone:

"I've had this message from Mum saying that Dad's not well and she's staying the night. What's going on?" I commenced.

"Where are you?" replied Pauline.

"At home," I stated.

"Daddy died at 5.25 this afternoon," said Pauline calmly.

I lost it, and started crying. It didn't last long, but it was a release of emotion at hearing about the death of a loved one. In addition, it was a shock as my father had been in such good form the day before.

My father had woken that day feeling ill. He was incontinent and having problems breathing. As the day wore on, he deteriorated still further and realised that he was dying. The hospital chaplain came to give him communion and the last rites, and shortly afterwards, his breathing became more laboured until his heart gave up, and he died. My mother explained to me the process in minute detail, from his struggling to breathe through to the body shaking violently as the brain shut down, and then to his last breath. By the time Christine had finished explaining it all, I was vicariously traumatised myself. She needed to tell me everything in order to come to terms with it herself.

My sister Pauline also told me that at one point a nurse had approached her to ask her whether they should give my father diamorphine 'to ease his path.' Pauline indicated to the nurse that this would be a good idea, but he had died before the drug could be administered.

My father had shown tremendous grace and selflessness in the face of death, which made it easier for those of us around him. He had always approached his illness with honesty and realism, protecting those around him as much as possible. This had been very different to the way Marie-Hélène and her family approached ill health. He had not lasted three months, but two weeks. He had gambled to extend his life by taking high doses of steroids, but his body could not take it. The steroids instead hastened his passing.

After we buried my father, I told Marie-Hélène that I wanted to split up, and would take her to France to live there. She took it a lot better than I thought she would. Her family were not happy with me, but my family understood. My sisters were particularly supportive as Marie-Hélène had never made much effort with them either before or after her illness. Pauline's husband Roger disapproved as he said I was abandoning an ill woman, and he had a point. However, I had somehow convinced myself that she was not as ill as in fact she was. She had time and again defied all medical expectations, so it seemed to me that she might live another twenty years. I had also given her the option of living in England with carers coming in to help her, but she had rejected that option.

She insisted that Scott was coming to France to live with her and I agreed as I was working full-time and did not want him to be on his own during the day. Besides, Scott was her dog – we had bought him to aid her recovery, so it was right that he stayed with her.

I did not manage our split very well, and still regret that I did it in such a short space of time. However, I was mourning my father and really was not coping very well with life at the time. In hindsight, I could have done it incrementally, and gradually let her spend more and more time in France until staying there permanently became an inevitable and obvious choice. However, I am not the Machiavellian type – once I had made the decision that this was the right thing to do, I was open and honest about it.

When I took Marie-Hélène to France for the last time, it was not easy. Her family were understandably hostile, and after unloading her luggage, I made a rapid retreat. I knew that I had made the right decision for both of us, but felt guilty at how I had done it. There was no sense of happiness when I got home. I was sad and fell into a depression for three months afterwards.

CHAPTER 16

A BEGINNING AND AN END

"You're always you, and that don't change, and you're always changing, and there's nothing you can do about it."

Neil Gaiman

During those first months of being separated from Marie-Hélène, I felt a mixture of emotions, but the overwhelming one was a sense of sadness. It had been my choice to split up, and I was sure that it was the right decision. However, it still had a profound emotional impact on me. It felt like the end of something, but at the same time not an end. We had no plans to get divorced, and I hoped that once the dust had settled, I would be able to visit her in France.

After a while, I began to feel an acute sense of loneliness. However, there was no going back. I missed Marie-Hélène but I did not miss her family, and I had burned my boats with them. I decided that I had to try to move on and that meant in my mind one thing - internet dating. At that time, the main site for dating was 'Match.com'. This site still exists but is now called simply 'Match.' Internet dating was still very much in its infancy in 2004, and not the normal way for couples to meet, but it was rapidly becoming popular and it seemed to me an ideal way of meeting new people.

I set up a Match.com profile in which I tried to be as honest as I could, except for the fact that I did not admit to smoking nor that I drank more alcohol than I should. I also might have exaggerated my height slightly by saying I was 5 foot 10 inches when in fact I was 5 foot 9½ inches. I have of course shrunk since and am now more like 5 foot 9. I included my hobbies and cultural interests, and tried to present myself as just a decent, caring person. I added a photo that made me look thinner than the overweight bloke that I was and am.

I was surprised when quite a few women responded to my profile and initiated conversations with me. I went on one date with a local teacher who on paper was a great match for me, but there was just not the right chemistry between us. However, there was one woman with whom I struck up a good relationship straight away. Her name was 'Lisa', and when she 'winked' at me electronically, I responded with a friendly email introducing myself, and asking her to tell me more about herself. After a short while, we dispensed with our aliases and Match.com email accounts and started communicating using our personal email addresses. I told her my full name and emphasised the aptronymic quality of the surname 'King' for someone who was a History teacher. She came straight back with:

"If you want to get in a contest for the silliest surname competition I think I win!"

Her surname was 'Onions' and she worked in the food industry. I knew from then on that we would get on well, for we had already struck up a relationship full of jokes and banter.

After a few weeks of emailing, Lisa and I started talking on the phone. She had a silky-smooth voice and our conversations were easy – we talked naturally and honestly. We then decided to meet up. The convention with internet dating is to meet in a public place, so we chose 'The Queen's Head' public house in Forest Hill for our first meeting. I was excited and a little bit nervous at the prospect of meeting Lisa for the first time. She was the same. I need not have worried - as soon as we met, any tensions or nervousness that we might have had evaporated, and within five minutes I felt as if I had known Lisa Onions all my life.

Over the following weeks and months, our relationship developed and we fell increasingly in love with each other. We found common interests in travel and food and wine. We disagreed about religion and politics but our discussions on these matters were open and honest. We would listen to each other's points of view and often found a surprising amount of common ground once we had explored the areas we disagreed about. We were only nine months difference in age, and shared a lot of cultural interests in terms of our memories of British film, music and television. For instance, Lisa was a huge fan of the film, 'Jaws' and could recount the script verbatim. I also loved the film, and we both had memories of it being in the cinemas in 1975. I saw it at the cinema with my family and enjoyed it, although my sister Elizabeth had nightmares for two weeks afterwards. Lisa was deemed by her parents too young for 'Jaws', and remembers having to glean the details of the film from her older brother Mark, who was allowed to see it.

My private life was turning round for the better, but my work life was getting more difficult. By 2005, it was becoming obvious that the independent school where I taught was struggling. Student numbers at St Patrick's School were down, and we were having to make staff redundant to keep the ship afloat. The main problem was that the school was being squeezed in a market where there was more supply than demand. Other girls' schools in the area were more popular, so we were struggling to compete. Ironically, our academic results were improving, but with an expensive, large nineteenth century building to maintain, our finances were falling below the level required to remain solvent. I was finding work increasingly stressful, so was glad that my private life was improving.

However, I got word from Marie-Hélène's family that her health was deteriorating. I had lost touch and was unaware that she had spent time in hospital, that a shunt had been put in her brain and that she was losing the ability to walk. I went to see her in France and she was pleased to see me, as indeed was Scott, who jumped all over me lovingly.

Marie-Hélène's family was less happy to see me and made it known to me. I was accused of being a coward, and of abandoning her, and these allegations hurt. They were even angrier when I pointed out that in many ways it was me that had been abandoned, how they had never shown any concern for my welfare, and how it was Marie-Hélène who had chosen to be treated in France, and spend most of her time with them, not me. I was also not happy that I had not been kept up to date with the state of Marie-Hélène's health, as I would have visited her in hospital had I known that she was there.

Marie-Hélène's health deteriorated still further when her brain tumour came back and she needed chemotherapy. Once again, it took a while before I found out about it. By 2007, her health had declined to such an extent that she was confined to a wheelchair. I went to see her when she was staying in Maidstone with her sister and Paul, and we got on remarkably well. She had reverted to a childlike state and I found her incredibly sweet. It made me realise that had I managed her family better, I could have been more intimately involved in her care during that period of time.

In 2007, St Patrick's School finally went under. There had been attempts at rescuing it, but none had succeeded, so the bank called in its debts. It was very sad to see the demise of a school that had been so caring and been a happy learning environment for generations of girls. I had been there seven years and like everyone else was made redundant. It took me very little time to my job as Head of History and Philosophy at Farlbridge School in Kent. I was grateful to have a new challenge in a well-established independent school, which was in no danger of closing.

In the spring of 2008, Marie-Hélène's sister Béatrice contacted me to tell me that Marie-Hélène's health was declining further and that my wife wanted to have more contact with me. She suggested that I ring Marie-Hélène on a regular basis. I was happy to do this, so started ringing her weekly and sending her the occasional card. This was valuable contact; Marie-Hélène seemed to appreciate our communication. It was always difficult ringing, because I would say simply 'Bonjour, c'est Charles,' when the phone was answered, and whoever was on the other end would not even bother with a warm greeting, but simply pass me straight over to my wife. Our conversations were generally simple and affectionate, and Marie-Hélène would giggle at the slightest things. I would talk about past experiences that we shared, recounting incidents that were funny or bizarre. I found this rapprochement with Marie-Hélène cathartic and for the first time in years, believed that I was able to make a positive difference in her life.

These phone calls became more difficult over time as Marie-Hélène was losing the power of speech. One week in June 2008 I rang her and was greeted by a family member who told me that Marie-Hélène did not say much anymore. The conversation consisted of me trying to talk and a silence from Marie-Hélène on the other end. This was distressing, but I kept calm and promised her I would visit her soon. With the summer holidays rapidly approaching, I thought that might present an opportunity to see her. In the event I did not, to my shame, make the time or effort to visit Marie-Hélène in the summer of 2008. I had been accused of cowardice before, but this time I was a coward for I did not want to face the hostility of her family once again. I regret the fact that I failed to keep my word and make the trip over to France.

*****

It was the afternoon of Sunday 7th September 2008 when I got the phone call. I was outside the front of Lisa's house in Forest Hill painting the front entrance. I had moved in with her the previous year just before starting my job at Farlbridge School.

"It's your sister-in-law," said Lisa grimly after answering the phone and passing it to me. She had already guessed what the phone call was about.

Béatrice had called to tell me that Marie-Hélène was in hospital and had only been given a short time to live. I only had one question:

"Is she conscious?"

"Sometimes" replied Béatrice.

"I will come straightaway," I said.

My overriding concern was that Marie-Hélène would know I was with her as she went through the dying process. I also wanted to say goodbye to her properly. I phoned the Head of Farlbridge School, Liam Arnott, explained the situation, and he kindly gave me compassionate leave. I booked a Channel Tunnel ticket, packed quickly, got in my car and headed down to the CHRU (regional hospital) in Lille. I got there at about 8pm.

Marie-Hélène was in a private room, hooked up to a drip. Her breathing was laboured and she was asleep when I arrived. She looked very ill. I started crying as I saw her there, looking worse than I had ever seen her before. It was desperately sad.

Marie-Hélène's sister Béatrice explained to me that she had been admitted to hospital eight days before. I was annoyed that I had not been told earlier about her hospitalisation but kept my thoughts to myself. I had a fleetingly cynical thought that I had only been contacted now because they knew she was about to die and needed me to pay for the funeral. The priority was to focus solely on Marie-Hélène, and not embroil myself in arguments or recriminations. The room had a spare bed, so I settled down for the night using the bedclothes I had grabbed from home. I was relieved that I was there and hoped that Marie-Hélène would be conscious enough the next day, to know that I was with her.

In the morning, she was a little bit more alert and opened her eyes. I talked to her and held her hand, but there did not seem to be much response. She was drifting in and out of consciousness. Her oncologist, Dr Dubois, arrived and told me that she was going to be moved to a hospice where she would receive excellent end-of-life palliative care. The hospice was a specially designed unit attached to the main hospital, where a partner could stay with his or her loved one, and at the same time be supported by an in-house counsellor.

In order to move Marie-Hélène to the hospice unit, it was necessary to wheel her into a lift, take her down to another level, and then transport her a short distance. I stayed with her during the transfer and was relieved when at one point, she opened her eyes, looked me straight in the face, and squeezed my hand. This is what I had hoped for - we were reunited for one brief moment that I believe brought her comfort. She visibly relaxed after this, closed her eyes, and never regained consciousness.

Marie-Hélène was not expected to live more than a few days, but she was only forty-five years old and had a strong heart. Although she was in a deep coma, her body fought against the ravages of the cancer that had consumed her brain. I stayed with her all that week, until Friday, at which point I went home for the weekend to get some respite from the emotional toll.

I went back the following Monday to be with her once again. I was absent from work, but at that moment in time only one thing mattered – Marie-Hélène. The physical process of her dying was at times messy and noisy. She would cough up a red mixture of what seemed to me was blood and bile although my medical knowledge is limited. Her kidneys stopped functioning and her urine became the colour of blood. On the Monday night after I returned, she started making disturbing, primeval noises. It was so loud that the nurses became upset by it and called the duty doctor. I just said to him:

"This is really distressing."

"Above all, for her!" He replied.

I hoped he was wrong. It seemed to me that she was no longer in a state of consciousness at all. Her pupils had stopped responding to light, and there was no sign that she aware of what was going on.

I wondered in fact whether her soul had left her body shortly after she was moved to the hospice. The day after, Béatrice had arranged a visit from the chaplaincy staff. A very kind woman arrived and prayed for Marie-Hélène's safe passage to the afterlife. She prayed for her family, for Béatrice and for me. It was extremely moving and Marie-Hélène looked serene as she lay on her bed, seemingly unaware of what was going on. Shortly afterwards, Béatrice and I saw a pigeon outside the window of Marie-Hélène's room, and it seemed to be staring at us beatifically. We both noticed it independently and speculated whether it represented the spirit of Marie-Hélène moving on. We never saw it again.

By Wednesday of her second week in the hospice, Marie-Hélène's breathing became weaker and her face turned pale white. It was obvious that she was close to death. That night, Béatrice asked to be with her, so I gave up my bedside vigil to let her spend the final hours with Marie-Hélène.

I went home, knowing that it had been a privilege to be with Marie-Hélène during those ten days. However, I was exhausted and traumatised. I rang Béatrice early the following day and she informed me that Marie-Hélène had passed away at 5.30am in the morning. I was relieved it was all over. Later, I wrote a short poem to sum up my experience of those last few days:

Last Days

The vigil ensues,
The end of a play -
A final act with several scenes;
The body's terminality.

The noise is like
A stark symphony
Of rattling mouth with
Intense cacophony.

The finale of rasping
Reaches crescendo;
Decibels speaking
Of primal physicality.

At last the noise subsides
As breaths decrease.
And then the final phrase
Brings ultimate relief.

The day after Marie-Hélène died, I went back to France to see her at the family house in Bruay. Marie-Hélène was laid out in the same room as her father had been placed twelve years earlier when he passed away. It was extremely emotional seeing her dead, dressed and wearing make-up. I wept loudly, distraught with grief, guilt, and sadness. I needed that moment to let the emotions out. Marie-Hélène's mother came in whilst I was in melt-down, which annoyed me, but also made me get a grip on my emotions.

"She looks beautiful!" observed Sophie.

"Yes, but she never wore make-up like that." I replied.

Marie-Hélène was recognisable, but she had foundation and rouge on with bright red lipstick. This gave her the appearance of being a doll in my mind, a far cry from the Marie-Hélène I had known in life, who only ever used make-up sparingly. She had good skin and was naturally beautiful, so make-up was not something that she particularly needed. I was bothered by this because I felt it was a dishonest portrayal of who she had been in life. But of course, the undertakers had not known her, so just did their best to make her look beautiful in the way that they saw fit.

We discussed funeral arrangements. Béatrice was organising it and everything proved uncontentious until I mentioned that my mother and sister would be attending.

"No, we don't want any of your family at the funeral. It's their fault you and Marie-Hélène separated," said my mother-in-law firmly.

I was stunned. I had always experienced funerals to be a moment when a life was celebrated and those who knew that person came together without rancour. And in addition, we were arranging a public funeral, having invited not just close friends and family, but distant cousins and former colleagues of Marie-Hélène's. I knew that Marie-Hélène and her family were not particularly interested in members of my family, but I had no idea that they felt animosity towards them. In my mind, Sophie was being needlessly cruel.

I thought about telling my sister Elizabeth and my mother to come anyway - I could have done with their support. But in the end, I wanted Marie-Hélène's family to be able to grieve without any distractions or friction, so attended the funeral on my own.

The funeral was a fitting tribute to Marie-Hélène with songs, poems and readings that reflected her past and personality. Just as had been the case with her father's funeral, the men and women sat on separate sides of the church. But, that seemed of no consequence as I was feeling so isolated and wretched, that it did not really matter to me who I sat next to. I was overwhelmed by grief but managed for most of the service to hold it in. However, it was a funeral mass, and when all Marie-Hélène's former colleagues and friends came up to the front to say goodbye to her and receive communion, I finally cracked, and the tears flowed liberally.

After the funeral service, the burial was a distressing finale to what had been a good life, lived honestly , but cut off all too soon. I once again lost my composure as the coffin was lowered into the grave. I was comforted by Marie-Hélène's cousin, a relative I had always found understanding and compassionate. I then briefly attended the wake at the family house in Bruay with Scott affectionately jumping all over me, now without his mistress. The lifespan of dogs seems cruelly short, yet there is something particularly poignant and sad about a dog outliving its owner.

I chatted with Marie-Hélène's friend Wendy who had been an important person in our lives when we met in Peterhampton:

"We were young, discovering the world, and trying to make sense of it," I said, "Without Marie-Hélène our young adult lives would have been impoverished – she was so vibrant, funny and go-get-it."

Then I thought of what had happened in the subsequent years. When I had first met Marie-Hélène, she had been a very young looking, green-bespectacled woman with bags of energy. Illness had stolen her youth and concertinaed her life in a cruel way. Events had formed us, shook us, and taken us on a tortuous journey. It was a journey that had lasted exactly twenty years. I met Marie-Hélène on the 24th September 1988 and buried her on the 24th September 2008.

CHAPTER 17

CONTAINMENT

"Start with the end in mind."

Stephen R Covey, The 7 Habits of Highly Effective People

I went back to school in January 2014 with the knowledge that I had cocked up badly by sending Sofia a 'love' message. However, I had apologised and believed that she had enough residual regard for me not to use the message against me. I felt sorry that I had upset her, but in my apology I had explained that it was not her fault, but entirely due to problems I was having. Of course, I had no idea my imessage had never arrived.

On Friday 17th January I was five minutes away from the end of my teaching day when the Deputy Head of Farlbridge School, Robert Cook, turned up at my classroom.

"I need you to come with me now to see Liam," he said.

I knew what it was about as soon as he turned up at my door. I quickly dismissed the class and followed him to Liam Arnott's office. As I walked like a condemned man to the Headmaster's office all I could think was, 'This is it then, I'm going to be sacked.' I just hoped it was quick. I was not going to fight my dismissal as I had already realised that my message to Sofia had been gross misconduct. Yes, she had left the school and was an adult, but my message was not consistent with the professional standards of a teacher given the reaction it had received.

Liam took little time to get to the point:

"I've been talking to Mrs Messina this afternoon. Is it true that you sent Sofia an inappropriate message?"

"Yes, I did."

Liam consulted his notes and said, "Did it say 'I can't stop loving you Sofia?'"

"Yes, it was something like that. It wasn't good."

"Were you drunk at the time?"

"No, I was sober. It was a mental breakdown." I felt the walls closing in on me and my world falling apart. I had no desire to talk about my mid-life crisis with my boss; it was utterly humiliating.

"Are you going to suspend me?" I asked Mr Arnott.

"Don't tempt me," he replied.

"Do you want me to resign?" I asked. I was ready and willing to jump ship.

"We'll see about that."

"Look, I am having counselling. Mrs Messina contacted me soon afterwards and made me realise I'd lost the plot. She asked me to send her an apology, which I sent the same day."

"Well, it looks like she never got it."

I was filled with horror at the thought that Mrs Messina had never got my apology. I had promised her I would send it.

She must have spent three weeks expecting me to deliver on my promise and in her mind I hadn't. The poor woman – no wonder she had approached the school about it! This was getting worse by the second - I was feeling physically sick.

"Have you done anything criminal?" asked Liam

"No, I've done nothing illegal," I replied.

"What about inviting Sofia and Lucy out for lunch?"

"Yes, I did that, but there's nothing illegal about inviting people out to celebrate their exam success. Anyway, it never happened."

"What about other people's exam success – how were you going to celebrate theirs?"

"Look, I'd developed a friendship with Sofia and Lucy when they were at school, so I treated them differently, but, yes, I shouldn't have made that invitation. I can see how it looks."

"And what about this Facebook group you set up for ex-pupils?"

"Some ex-pupils came to see me, we took some selfies, and the easiest way to send them the photos was to set up the group. I'm happy to show it to you on Facebook."

"So when did you ask Sofia to be a friend on Facebook?"

"She sent me a friendship request back in June and I accepted it. I've always been happy to accept friendship requests from former students. I blocked her in October because I was having romantic feelings towards her, and then re-friended her just before I sent her that 'love' message."

"Did you exchange a lot of messages with her on Facebook?"

"We exchanged a few, but none of them was anywhere near as bad as that last message. I understand why she blocked me – it was gross misconduct… I know that. Look, I know how awful this thing is – may be I should talk to my wife about it."

"Don't" said Liam instinctively. I did not interpret this as an instruction to hide what I had done from my wife, but a very understandable reaction from someone who wanted to keep the incident quiet. It was the first hint of how this episode was going to be dealt with.

The conversation soon changed to what would happen next. It was the second evening of the Staff Pantomime, and I was in no mood to get on stage and prance around. My thoughts were directed at 'doing a runner.' In my mind, I knew where I would go. There was a Franciscan priory which I had once visited, where I was sure I would be taken in and given some spiritual guidance. Yes, I had reached rock bottom, and a retreat was the only thing for it.

"We will carry on as normal," said Liam. "We need you to be at the staff pantomime tonight, being a pirate."

"Really, I don't feel up to it. I'd rather not, and frankly I'm not sure it's worth me coming back to work on Monday."

"Yes, Charles," said Robert, the Deputy Head who was also a great thespian, "I will play Captain Hook, and I'm sure you'll be fine when you get on stage."

"The other thing we need you to do is to write up your version of what happened," said Liam.

"I can do that now if you like," I said.

"No, take your time, and we'll meet again on Monday after the Head of Departments' meeting. Oh yes, and please don't have any contact with Sofia or her family."

"I wasn't intending to, but I do feel terrible that Mrs Messina never got my apology."

"We can sort out an apology shortly, but in the meantime, let us deal with the Messinas. Now are you going to be okay?" asked Liam.

"No, I'm not going to be alright," I answered truthfully. I felt like I was going to crack at any moment.

"There is support for you. Daniel Bennett was the first person Mrs Messina approached about this, so you can phone him over the weekend. He'll be supportive."

The meeting concluded and I went back to my office. I was in turmoil as I reflected on the car crash that I had created. I was still considering doing a runner but yet I got the impression that Liam was going to fix this, and there was no sign that I was going to be asked to resign. Yet, it occurred to me that resignation would not be such a bad course of action. I had been thinking about leaving teaching for several months and had built up enough wealth to fund an early retirement, so why not? Yet, if we could contain this, and I could avoid hurting my wife by telling her about it, then perhaps I should stick around.

Whilst I was having these thoughts, Robert Cook turned up at my office for a chat. He started by saying:

"I know people who have done some pretty bad things who are still in this school."

"What? As bad as what I've done?"

"Yes, and they've moved on from those things."

"You mean, you think I can survive this?"

"Yes."

"But I'm assuming I will have to go through some sort of disciplinary process. It is pretty bad."

"Not necessarily."

I was astonished. I had done something that was clearly gross misconduct, yet it seemed possible that I would not be disciplined for it.

"But I've got to get a warning at least," I said. It seemed counter intuitive to think otherwise.

I was grateful to Robert for coming to see me. He and Liam had realized I was emotionally unstable and were doing their best to keep me together. I started to analyse what had happened in the meeting. Liam had interrogated me quite aggressively to begin with and obviously wanted to rule out the possibility that I had done something criminal that would hurt the school. Once, he was persuaded that what I had done was manageable, he was now going to fix it and make sure that as few people knew as possible. It seemed to me a sensible way to approach what had happened, and I appreciated the support. I felt the best thing was to do what I was told and take my lead from Liam.

I knew then that I had to pull myself together, do the pantomime, and then go home, pretending to my wife that everything was alright. So, that is exactly what I did. I hated every moment of the pantomime that evening.

*****

The following Monday we met again and I handed over my statement explaining a time line of events and personal background. Liam had taken legal advice since our previous meeting. The advice was that he had to do a disciplinary procedure with me, which came as no surprise.

"Who's going to the disciplinary?" I asked

"I will do it, but it won't end in termination," he replied.

I was mightily relieved and grateful to Liam for taking a worry of my mind. I knew what he was proposing was completely against proper procedure in that an investigating officer should not be on a decision-making panel, and even more extraordinarily, should not be the sole person on the panel. In criminal law it would be akin to the investigating Police Officer going on to be the judge in a case. However, Liam was showing me compassion and keeping me on side, as well as containing the bad news that I had created. I was happy to go along with the strategy that had been devised, and furthermore it meant that I would be able to spare my wife the hurt of admitting my emotional infidelity. I was therefore keen that any paperwork associated with this issue would be given to me at school rather than posted home!

Liam told me to write an apology for Mrs Messina that she could show to Sofia. I agreed to meet him in his office first thing the following morning in order to send it. Liam advised me to keep it fairly short. I wanted to write something heartfelt as I was painfully aware that I had upset Sofia and her mother badly. As I had already sent one apology, it did not take me long to come up with a form of wording for my second apology that reflected my genuine feelings:

"Dear Mrs Messina, I am extremely sorry for expressing feelings towards Sofia that I should not have had. My deepest regret is the distress that I have caused Sofia and you. Please reassure Sofia that I will not be contacting her again and I hope this episode does not destroy the good memories that she has of the school. I wish her all the very best for the future. I tried to send an apology to you last month but it did not arrive, so please accept my sincere and deepest apologies now. Regards, Charles King."

The following morning I sent the apology as an imessage to Mrs Messina in front of Liam Arnott. He saw me press the 'send' button. He said to me:

"I'm going to make this one go away," a comment that I appreciated. He was really doing his best for me, and I was grateful.

I then emailed him a screenshot of it. Once again, just as with my first apology, the imessage failed to arrive. When Mrs Messina contacted Liam about it at lunchtime, he asked me to send it again, so I sent it as a text message instead. I am assuming that she then received it.

I requested that the disciplinary be delayed for personal reasons, so that I could have some breathing space from the crisis I had created. My counselling was going well and I was thinking that perhaps we were turning a corner. Yet, there was one comment that had been made at my meetings with Liam and Robert that kept on coming back in my mind. Robert had commented that my message to Sofia had been 'self-destructive'. He was right – it had been self-destructive but I did not know why.

*****

It was another month before the disciplinary took place. Liam telephoned me during half-term and told me it would be on Wednesday 26th February 2014. He also gave me a standard letter about the disciplinary which said I had a right to be accompanied by a representative. Seeing as he had already told me I was not going to be sacked, and the strategy was to restrict the number of people who knew about the episode, I decided the most helpful thing would be to turn up unaccompanied.

I was nervous about the disciplinary as it was another reminder of what an idiot I had been, and I had to talk once again about deeply personal feelings. Liam realised this and was very kind. He started off by giving some background to what I had done and told me that Sofia was now having counselling. 'That makes two of us,' I thought to myself. He asked me predictable questions about whether I considered the message inappropriate, what my feelings for Sofia had been when she had been a pupil at the school and whether I wanted to stay at the school. I told him that I recognised what I had done had been unprofessional, that I had been fond of Sofia as a pupil, and that I did want to stay at the school. I explained the mitigating circumstances that had led to my message, admitted that I had been deluded and that it had not been 'my finest hour'.

The most difficult question that Liam asked me was what I would have done if Sofia had responded positively to my message. I answered that I didn't know as it had thankfully never come to that. At the end of the meeting, he asked me if I had anything else I wanted to say. I paused for a moment as I reflected on what he wanted me to say. I thought he was encouraging me to give further mitigation, so I talked about my counselling and how the trauma and guilt associated with my first wife's death had affected me negatively.

The meeting was short and at the end of it Liam told me what I was expecting - he was going to give me a final written warning. He had already told me in the meeting that we needed 'to close all of this', so it was clear to me it was time to wrap this one up and move on.

I was glad that the matter had been dealt with so compassionately and was determined that I would not let anything like it happen again. Liam and Robert had looked after me and I was keen to repay them by doing a top job. However, one thing still bothered me. Sofia's father did not know about what had happened. If he were to find out, it occurred to me the Messinas could prove difficult in the future. I had an uncomfortable feeling that despite my best efforts at heartfelt apologies, Mr Messina would not be as compassionate as his wife.

CHAPTER 18

LISA

"As usual, there is a great woman behind every idiot."
John Lennon

I was in a state of grief for some time after Marie-Hélène died. I went back to work immediately after she passed away as Liam Arnott was concerned that I had been away from school too long. I was, however, given compassionate leave for the day of her funeral. On the Saturday after her burial, I had an Open Day, and a month after Marie-Hélène's death in October 2008, I led an overseas trip to Berlin, Krakow and Prague. It was good that work took me away from my grief and made me focus on others rather than myself.

However, it was not easy. As part of our visit to Krakow, I had organised a trip to Auschwitz, an excursion that really tested my mental health when I had been through so many emotions, so recently. My own suffering made me acutely sensitive to the horrors at Auschwitz, something that had not happened on my previous visit. Perhaps, I should have counted myself fortunate that I had not suffered such extreme trauma as those persecuted by the Nazis, but instead I just felt vulnerable and emotional. It was a difficult trip and I was relieved when we got back. In November I returned to work after half-term at a low ebb, and it was at this time that I first started to teach ICT to a young Sofia Messina.

Of course, I put on a brave face and just tried to carry on as normal. However, I was withdrawn and unsociable for several months, and knew that I needed some kind of psychological support. I therefore arranged through my friend and colleague, Stephen Grant, the Chaplain, to see the school counsellor. I had five 40-minute sessions with her and found it very useful. However, she suddenly left the school for a reason completely unconnected to the fact that she was counselling me! I felt I had made enough progress to carry on without support, so did not have any more therapy. I now realise with hindsight that I should have continued with some further counselling.

The first year after Marie-Hélène died was very difficult, but I got through it due to one person. That person was Lisa Onions. Lisa knew I was suffering, but tolerated my insularity and my alcohol related self-medication, and gently tried to get me to talk about how I felt. There were one or two occasions when I found myself crying on her shoulder, yet I found it hard to put it all into words. I felt a moral failure at having separated from Marie-Hélène and for alienating her family so completely. I felt guilt at not supporting her as well as I should have done and not loving her as much as she loved me. I still had an irrational thought that I had been in part responsible for her brain cancer. I also felt that a part of me had died with Marie-Hélène, and that death was in a very real sense my nearest neighbour. My job, and all the petty politics and rules connected with it seemed ridiculous and insignificant in comparison.

So Lisa became my rock – a reassuring presence and a listening ear even if I did not talk as much as I should have done. Of course, Lisa was suffering too – she saw my pain and felt it. She also had to now cope with the fact that Marie-Hélène was dead, and dead people are impossible to live up to. The dead can do no wrong and there is a danger that we idolise the dead or love them more when they are dead than we did when they were alive. Loving a dead person is easy, for they can become in your mind whatever you want them to be, and they will never disappoint you! I was of course keen to avoid doing this, but in my grief, I think I tended to be too hard on myself and may be imagine that Marie-Hélène had been a much better person than me. The truth is, of course, that she was a normal, flawed individual with strengths and weaknesses, just like all good people.

The other way in which Lisa helped me, was to get me focused on our future together. On Valentine's Day in 2009 we got engaged. Lisa told me to propose to her, so I did. She accepted, which was not a surprise given that she had told me to ask for her hand in marriage. It was, in reality, a joint decision as we had been together over four years and both of us were keen to make a long-term future together. We bought her engagement ring together, which meant that we jointly went shopping for it, she chose it, and I paid for it.

Once we had got officially engaged, we then started planning what sort of marriage we wanted and where it was to be held. Not being a religious person, Lisa wanted a registry office wedding, whereas I argued for a church wedding. Lisa said that the marriage was about us and not

God, whereas my argument was that a church wedding gave us more flexibility. In a civil wedding, one is not allowed to display any religious symbols, mention God, sing hymns with a religious content or refer to anything divine. One can talk about love, commitment, and other non-religious abstract concepts, but one cannot cross over into using abstract religious language. I respected Lisa's religious scepticism but, as the son of Welsh parents, I did not see why I should be denied singing 'Bread of Heaven' at the wedding!

Lisa relented and saw the advantages of being able to mix secular and religious readings as well as religious and non-religious songs. So she agreed to having a church wedding. We then had to decide on a venue.

We did not want a big church, as it was not going to be a large wedding. I had quite a small family, and Lisa a smaller one. Even with all our friends and close colleagues, we only needed a church that seated 150 people, so we opted for the School Chapel at Farlbridge School where I was Head of History and Philosophy. It seemed an ideal choice especially as I could then ask my friend Stephen, the Chaplain, to officiate at the wedding on his home turf.

Having decided on the religious venue, we then had to choose a place for the reception. We visited different hotels, golf courses and restaurants, but there was only one place that caught our imagination – Bigsbury Park, near Rainham. With beautiful gardens, an orangery and a stylishly converted barn, it had just the atmosphere we were looking for. When we went to visit it, we took Lisa's friend Zoe with us who had come over to stay from Ireland. She was heavily pregnant with her third child at the time, and after the Bigsbury Park Representative had spent about fifteen minutes addressing her explanations primarily at Zoe, we realised that she was a little confused about who I was marrying.

We planned the wedding meticulously and the day passed off extremely well. Our guests had a great time, the food was excellent, and we had speeches, which contained the usual mix of satire and bawdy humour.

So, in August 2010, I found myself married once more, but this time to someone who was not popping off for weeks at a time to a foreign country. It felt like a resurrection of types, as if I had been given a second chance at life, and I was determined that I would make a better fist of my second marriage than I had of my first. I had married a woman who was amazing in so many ways – beautiful, intelligent, incredibly kind and side-splittingly funny. Lisa is one of the wittiest people I have ever met, and takes the mickey out of me mercilessly, something that is necessary to prick the balloon of my pomposity. Of course, she is not perfect. She is capricious; loving and kind one moment, and then negative and horrible if something annoys her. That something is usually me. Lisa suffers in these darker instances from what we call 'Nastiness Tourettes,' liberally slinging insults in my direction. She is in the long-term, a very tolerant and patient person but in the short-term is the exact opposite, getting frustrated at a lack of progress or the inability to get instant results. For instance, she is learning to drive at the moment and gets very frustrated that she cannot master all the associated skills straight away. I am superficially the complete opposite – generally laid back and patient, rarely getting angry or frustrated. In the professional life of a teacher, one has to develop these qualities to survive.

Yet, despite marrying a wonderful and exceptional human being, and having the best of intentions, I struggled to adjust to married life again. At the heart of this was not just a tendency towards selfishness and thoughtlessness, but the deep-seated unresolved guilt and trauma that I felt surrounding the illness and death of Marie-Hélène. I had been wounded badly and had a handicap – not a physical disability that would be obvious for people to see, but an emotional handicap that meant I was holding in a whole load of extreme emotions that were bursting to get out. I was like Champagne that had been shaken up but held in by a cork, a cork that had been unwrapped, but not yet released from the neck of the bottle. Rather than addressing this psychological elephant in the room, I would direct my energies towards my work, which was becoming increasingly important to me again after the initial period following Marie-Hélène's death. I was also developing a wider circle of friends and socialising more.

There was also the issue that I had never had a real marriage before. For much of my time with Marie-Hélène, she had not been around, so I maintained more or less the life of a bachelor even though I was married. Lisa wanted us to be a conventional married couple, and this was new to me.

So it was, that for the first three and half-years of my marriage to Lisa, I was not a great husband, and it is remarkable that she put up with my selfish ways and inattentiveness. It is a testament to her love for me that she did.

On the other hand, it was not all bad. We often had fun and made each other laugh, and we loved each other deeply. In addition, we had a common interest that always brought us close together. That interest was dogs.

We got our first dog in November 2007. One of Lisa's colleagues had a litter of seven Labrador-Retriever cross puppies, so when they were four weeks old we went over to see them and met their parents. None had yet been sold so we had the pick of the bunch. The mother was a beautiful Chocolate Labrador and the father a handsome Golden Retriever. The puppies were all incredibly cute and there was no doubt in our minds that one of them was going to find a home with us. All the puppies were black, but one of them had a particularly dark, shiny coat. She seemed bolder than the others, came up to us, and yapped. It was almost as if she had chosen us rather than the other way round. We had found our girl! We named her Betty and she joined us at home when she was a mere eight weeks old.

I had just started working at Farlbridge School when we got Betty, and had found out that the Bursar was a dog-lover and had kept a dog in one of the school residential buildings for several years until it had sadly died. The chaplain also kept a dog on site. So I asked the Bursar, who was in charge of health and safety, whether I could bring Betty to school with me every day and keep her in my office. He agreed, so our puppy came to school with me every morning for several months. Betty became quite an attraction, and I started up a puppy club, whereby dog-loving pupils would come along and play with her after school, whilst I went to meetings or caught up with my marking. Every lunchtime I would walk her round the school grounds, which gave me a break from the intensity of the job. It worked very well until the Head of the Junior School argued that Betty was a health and safety risk! When she was six months old, Betty was expelled from school and had to spend working hours at home. Lisa consequently decided to go part-time at work, so that Betty would not be on her own for too long during the day.

In 2009, two years after we had adopted Betty, we decided that it would be good for her to have a sister, so we got another dog. Preferring cross breeds to pedigrees, we went for a Cavalier King Charles Spaniel-Collie cross, which we named 'Lola'. Lola has a completely different personality to Betty. Whereas Betty is 'all-dog' - running after and retrieving balls and defending herself when aggressed by other dogs – Lola is half-dog, half-diva. She is incredibly sensitive. When Betty ran over Lola as a puppy, hurting her legs, she cried so much that we had to take her to the vets. At the vets, she yelped and screamed at the sight of a needle. It turned out there was nothing wrong with her. Lola constantly seeks attention and reassurance, whines about the slightest thing, and is scared of other dogs. She's amazing and is my favourite, if I'm allowed a favourite!

In November 2010, we saw a dog online that caught our attention. It was a Pug-Maltese Terrier cross. It was a very cute looking pug with long fluffy fur. Lisa urged me to get her, but I resisted, arguing that two dogs were more than enough. Then, one night, I had a dream that we had three dogs and life was wonderful. In my dream Lisa and I were in a park with the three dogs playing happily. The next day, I went and bought the Pug-Maltese Terrier cross that we had seen online. I took one look at it, fell instantly in love, and ten minutes later she was on the way home with me. We named her 'Poppy'. Our family was complete.

*****

Shortly after we got married, Lisa's father and stepmother moved out of South London to live in Lincolnshire near Lisa's stepsister and stepbrother. They bought a lovely house near Lincoln and were relieved to be out of their ever more crowded corner of the metropolis.

However, in the summer of 2011, Lisa's father, John, was diagnosed with bowel cancer at the age of 78. It felt like a cruel blow, given that he had only just moved into his new house and was enjoying the country life. He was in the early stages, so his consultant told him to consider an operation to treat the cancer. However, his health was such that there were considerable risks to surgery. He decided against any invasive procedure, and instead opted to have regular check-ups.

Lisa was very close to her father. She and he shared many personality traits including a natural charm and an astuteness about people they came into contact with. They also had a tendency to 'dog days' when they would for short periods fall into a state of depression. They could also both be quite tough on those closest to them, testing the patience of their respective spouses. Their bond was closer by the fact that Lisa was John's only child by blood. Lisa's older brother, Mark, had died of skin cancer at the age of 28, a family tragedy that had affected her and all her family profoundly. John rarely talked about it, perhaps because he found it too painful to recount.

By the autumn of 2012, John's condition had got worse and he commenced chemotherapy. His health continued to deteriorate despite the chemo, so Lisa was spending more and more time with him in Lincolnshire. It all felt depressingly familiar to me, and I dreaded the thought of losing another member of the family. By the spring of 2013, John's bowel cancer had advanced and spread, and he knew that he only had a short time to live. He celebrated his 80th birthday in March with the knowledge that it would be his last. Lisa was struggling to cope with what was happening, and I was still not emotionally strong enough to give her all the support she needed. When we stayed with John and Lisa's stepmother, I would withdraw into myself and play Scrabble on my phone or do crosswords. I was not very communicative. As I had not dealt with the trauma of my own past, I was not best placed to deal with Lisa's emotional turmoil. What was happening mirrored much of what I had experienced in the past, so it was, on a smaller scale, a bit like putting an untreated shell-shocked soldier back in the trenches. In addition, I was stressed out at work trying to deal with the constant demands being made on me by Sofia's year group as they approached their A Level examinations.

On 24th May, John died, peacefully at home. The Marie Curie nurses who supported him in his last days had been magnificent, reminding me once again of the amazing compassion of the medical profession. The funeral was a fitting celebration of his life.

The death of her father affected Lisa deeply, and she lost her motivation for work. She had been employed in Business Services at Clifford Chance in Canary Work for eleven years and was already losing interest in her job even before her father's illness. With the death of her father, any residual enthusiasm for work she had, finally evaporated. Lisa handed in her notice and retired at the beginning of October 2013. There were no money worries, so I was happy for her to spend more time at home if that is what she wanted.

Looking back, I can see that Lisa's grief had affected me much more profoundly than I realised at the time. My mental state was not helped by the poor examination results that summer and I was also deeply affected by the fifth anniversary of Marie-Hélène's death in September. In addition, as we approached Christmas, another personal tragedy started to unfold. My inappropriate message was about to be followed up with a situation that would once again test me emotionally; a situation that I'm not sure I would have got through if it had not been for counselling.

CHAPTER 19

CHRISTINE

"Just when you think it can't get any worse, it can. And just when you think it can't get any better, it can."

Nicholas Sparks, At First Sight

Before Christmas 2013, my sister Elizabeth rang me and told me that my mother, Christine, was not very well.

"She's not as mobile and a bit confused," she told me. I had not given my mother's health a lot of thought given the personal crisis I was going through. My mother was 77 years old and her mobility was not great – she was struggling to walk due to a degenerative bone condition in her back. She had also been diabetic for over thirty years.

In 2011, Christine had fallen in her house and, unable to get up or call for help, she had lain there for two days and lapsed into a diabetic coma. Eventually, a neighbour, realising something was wrong, alerted the emergency services who used an axe to break down her front door. She was barely alive when they found her, with a core body temperature of 29°c. Somehow, she had been brought back to life in hospital.

My mother's health was never as good after her near-death experience in 2011, but she did recover mentally, and maintained her joie de vivre. She was also fiercely independent. When, after her fall, she lost her ability to walk more than a few steps, she got herself a mobility scooter. This allowed her to go into town and visit her local friends. She told me that one evening she had taken her scooter to a dinner party, had consumed a skin full of wine, and then drunkenly and happily scootered her way home.

The last time I had seen her was at the end of October. I had taken my mother to see her good friends Patricia and Chris, who were also my godparents. We stayed overnight, and Christine had been her usual, controlling self, treating me like the teenager she had no idea I had regressed into in my feelings for Sofia! I remember her waking me up at 7.45am and telling me to get up for breakfast. I was not best amused. She also wound me up on the way home by telling me how to drive and by generally being her normal, objectionable self. Whilst I was at the wheel, I was so furious, I had a fleeting thought that it would not be so bad if I careered off the road, ran into a tree and killed both of us. My mother was a lovely person who never wished anyone harm, but she often did her best to disguise this loveliness.

Of course, I was her favourite as the only boy with two older sisters. She once said to me:

"Do you know what your sisters call you?"

"No, Mummy, what do they call me?"

"'Golden Boy'. They think you're my favourite, but of course I love you all equally."

The next time I talked to my sister Elizabeth, I asked her whether it was true that she and Pauline referred to me as 'Golden Boy.'

"No," she replied, "We call you 'Golden *Balls*...'"

*****

My sisters and I have a habit of rotating who hosts Christmas. So every three years Lisa and I invite my family over. It was our turn in 2013. On Christmas Day, my family arrived at about one o'clock. Elizabeth, and her two children, Jack and Louise turned up first. Elizabeth was as chatty as normal, barely breathing as a stream of consciousness spewed from her mouth. Within five minutes I had been told every detail of her day up to that point. Shortly afterwards, my other sister Pauline arrived with her husband Roger, their son Sebastien and our mother Christine.

I was shocked when I saw my mother. I had not seen her in two months, but it looked like she had aged five years. Her eyes were hollowed out, her complexion was grey, and she seemed to have shrunk another four inches from when I had taken her to see my godparents in October. She had also lost her 'bounce' and looked more vulnerable than I had encountered her before. I was upset for I knew instinctively that she was dying. I did my best not to show my emotions.

Mealtimes are always enjoyable when you are married to a trained chef, and Lisa enjoys cooking for others. She put her heart and soul into our 2013 family Christmas meal – it was delicious. Even my mother showed signs of her old self when she refused to have her large wine glass replaced with

169

a smaller one, and insisted on a top up of red. However, in other ways, she was far from normal. It was particularly worrying when, whilst I was sitting next to her, she said, "Where's Charles?"

After lunch, we did the traditional exchange of Christmas presents with those of us not driving indulging in further glasses of alcoholic beverages, whilst others drugged themselves up with coffee for the journey home.

In the evening, my sister Pauline left first with her family and my mother. Afterwards, I sat in the living room and wept in front of Elizabeth, and her grown up children, Jack and Louise. They seemed a little taken aback because they had never seen me cry before, but I was so upset by how much my mother had deteriorated, that I could not help myself.

"What's wrong with her?... I think she's dying," I sniffled.

"Yes, she's not going to celebrate another Christmas," commented Elizabeth matter-of-factly.

It was worrying and put my mid-life crisis in its proper perspective. Elizabeth and I discussed one thing that particularly disturbed us. My mother had been managing her diabetes brilliantly since she had been diagnosed in 1982. She injected herself with insulin four times a day, knowing exactly how much to take, and when to inject it. On Christmas Day 2013 she had forgotten to inject her insulin and did not seem that concerned about it. This made us wonder whether she had lost control of her diabetes in general. If that were the case, her life would indeed be in danger.

I next saw my mother on Sunday 19th January, two days after Liam and Robert had interviewed me about my inappropriate message. She did not look any better than she had done at Christmas and was complaining about a pain in her left leg. I was more concerned about how well my mother was looking after herself, so quizzed her about her diabetes. Fortunately, Pauline, who lived just half a mile away, had found Christine a carer who was coming in mornings and afternoons to prepare her meals and ensure she injected herself properly.

A week later, I got word that my mother had been admitted into hospital. She had a blocked artery in her left leg. I drove over to see her and found her in quite a confused state. Her leg did not look good and was cold to the touch. On the positive side, because she was in hospital, she was being looked after well and her diabetes was once more under control. However, the damage had been done – her circulation issue was a direct result of the problems in managing her diabetes. What was more puzzling was that I had no idea why her mind was so befuddled.

Within ten days the decision was made to amputate her left leg at the knee. The operation was scheduled for Tuesday 11th February. We were all shocked by the idea of our mother becoming an amputee, especially given the generally poor state of her health.

On the day of the operation, Elizabeth and I went to see Christine in the morning and promised her that we would stay with her until she came round from surgery. It was a nerve-racking wait, however Elizabeth cheered me up with a joke.

"I didn't want to tell Mummy this joke before the operation," said Elizabeth, "but I guess it's okay to tell you."

"Knock yourself out Liz – let's hear your joke."

"Okay, here goes. There's a woman who has just come round from having her leg amputated. After the operation, she's put back on the ward and the surgeon comes to see her. He says to her, "Do you want the good news or the bad news?" She says, "Give me the bad news first." The surgeon replies, "Well the bad news is that unfortunately we amputated the wrong leg, so we're going to have to take you back into surgery to cut off the other leg." The woman looks horrified but nevertheless has the curiosity to ask the surgeon, "So what's the good news?" The surgeon replies, "The good news is that the woman opposite you wants to buy your slippers!""

I laughed heartily despite it being a fairly average joke. Given our situation and our joint propensity for black humour, the joke gave us the light relief we needed. After I had stopped laughing, I commented:

"I'm glad you didn't tell Mummy that joke before the operation."

My mother took longer than expected to come round from the anaesthetic, so it was not until 8pm that Elizabeth and I were able to see her. She was conscious, but looked pale and exhausted. However, she was the most cogent I had seen her for weeks. We kissed her goodnight and went home. A few days later Elizabeth told Christine the amputation joke. Mother loved it!

*****

My mother's rehabilitation initially went as planned, so after 10 days she was transferred to a cottage hospital near to her house. However, after five days there, she was suddenly transferred back to the general hospital where her operation had taken place. She had kidney failure. Christine was given a bed in the Medical Assessment Unit and various tests were done. When the results came back, Pauline, Elizabeth and I were called into the hospital by a senior consultant.

"We're trying to get her kidneys working again," stated the consultant. "But if that doesn't work, she's going to need dialysis."

We were fully expecting the consultant to tell us this, so we talked about where dialysis would take place, and how often it would be needed.

"However, it may be that Christine does not live that long anyway," continued the consultant. "Our tests show that she has advanced endocrinal cancer."

We were shocked but not particularly surprised by this news, for we all suspected that there was something else going on. However, it did make us wonder whether they should have picked up her condition earlier. They had chopped the leg off a woman with terminal cancer without even knowing just how ill she was!

Within a week, Christine's kidneys started working again, and she was transferred out of the Medical Assessment Unit and on to a general ward. As we entered March, she seemed to be recovering from her amputation, and there was a brief moment when she improved enough to be wheeled round the corridors and have coffee in the hospital cafeteria. However, her cancer then advanced further and both her physical and mental well-being declined.

The most distressing part was watching my mother lose her mind. She had always been a highly intelligent, commanding presence, but as we progressed through March, she became more and more confused and paranoid. One afternoon when I visited her, she thought that the nurses were out to get her, and was convinced I had come in to take her home. She talked about her mother when she meant her daughter and had developed a fantasy that her husband was still alive. I tried to calm her but all she could say was, "You've got to get me fucking out of here" in a loud voice, much to my embarrassment. Nothing I said could calm her down, and I felt completely useless.

I eventually had to go home. Visiting her three times a week was taking up a lot of time and emotional energy, especially as it involved a 150-mile round journey. I was struggling to cope with the demands of my job and the challenges of her illness.

It was less traumatising when we got to the last stages of her life. By the beginning of April she was hardly eating anything, and had lost the energy to fight against her cancer or the hospital regime she so hated. She would spend more and more time sleeping, and was calmer when she spoke. The last few days were relatively peaceful, and she regressed into a childlike state asking for her 'Mummy.' The day she died, she uttered her last words before falling into a coma. These words were:

"The party's over!"

My mother lived her life to the full and always told a good story. She loved life and particularly enjoyed a good party. She was an avid Francophile, visiting France with my father two or three times a year for holidays, in which they would play boules with the locals and drink red wine. She also had a wicked sense of humour.

Christine once told me about an evening she had spent in a rural French restaurant. She and Philip had eaten well and drunk a fair amount of the local wine. They chatted amicably with the locals who were enjoying their company. Everyone was having such a ball that when it came to closing time, the owner locked the doors, and brought out extra wine to share for free with my parents and the few remaining diners. The atmosphere became more and more light-hearted.

"One of the men started chatting me up," my mother told me, "Your father was so kaylied, he didn't even notice."

With a twinkle in her eye, she told me that the old local chatting her up, had produced a condom and said to her grinning, "In France we call this 'la copote anglaise' " [Literally – the English hood].

Christine had smiled back and replied simply: "In England we call it 'une lettre française '"

She and my father had staggered out of the restaurant in the early hours, happy, but very much the worse for wear.

So for Christine, life really was a wonderful party, making her last words entirely appropriate. Elizabeth and I held our mother's hands as she died peacefully at 5.25pm on Wednesday 9th April 2014. It is a bizarre coincidence that my mother passed away at exactly the same time of day as my father. An hour later, Elizabeth and I went to a local pub and both ordered our mother's favourite aperitif – gin and tonic! It felt a fitting way to mark her passing from this world.

The funeral took place two weeks later. Christine had left instructions as to what she wanted in the service, including wording and hymns. Pauline, Elizabeth and I all did readings. She was buried in the same grave as her husband Philip. Just before he had died in 2004, he had told me and my sisters how proud he was of us all. My mother had also said she was proud of me a few months before her death. I couldn't help thinking, that if they were still alive, and had known about the mess I had recently created in my life, my parents may have taken a somewhat different view.

CHAPTER 20

'REVENGE'

"When a tree falls it resounds with a thundering crash; and
yet a whole forest grows in silence."

Jocelyn Murray

In May 2014 I had a successful professional review. My
reviewer did not know about my 'love' message to Sofia, but
my Head of House Daniel Bennett did. Daniel had given my
reviewer the normal positive feedback about my pastoral
skills. My reviewer had written, "He works hard on getting
his relationships with his tutees right as their tutor, and his
organisation and effort are much appreciated by DJB."
Daniel was going on sabbatical for the last six weeks of term,
so his Deputy was taking over the running of the House. I
was asked in turn to step in as Deputy Head of House for a
few weeks, which I was happy to do. I had put my previous
professional difficulties behind me and moved on.

It had been five months since my message to Sofia, and my
private life had improved as well. Yes, I was mourning my
mother but her death had been a relief as she was no longer
suffering. My counselling had helped me deal with it better
than I expected I would. Counselling was also helping me
to understand myself better. Most importantly, my
relationship with Lisa had improved considerably. My crisis

had made me realise just how much I loved her and how in the past I had neglected her and taken her for granted. With her being free from the stresses of work, and me focusing on her exclusively, we had grown closer to each other than ever before. And I had not burdened her with the hurt of telling her about Sofia. She had thankfully no idea how near we had come to disaster.

I had not had any contact with Sofia or her family, so assumed that they, like me, had now moved on from what I had done just before Christmas the previous year. It was therefore a surprise when, on Thursday 5th June, Robert Cook came to find me in my office. The Messinas had been in contact with Liam Arnott. I went to have a chat with Liam and Robert once again:

"It looks like things have changed," commenced Liam, "Sofia now knows that her Mum has talked to the school about your message, and Mr Messina now knows about it too."

My heart sank. This was not sounding good.

"It looks like they are now in a stage of 'anger'," he continued. My heart sank below my knees.

"Well, if they're so angry, I'm happy to meet with them. It might help them to direct their anger at me personally," I suggested. It was not something that would be easy for me but I have always been a believer in 'truth and reconciliation'. As part of that, having the opportunity to show your emotions at someone you are angry with, can be remarkably cathartic. I was also worried that my inability to communicate with them directly might have allowed them to imagine all kind of things about me that were not true. 'They probably think I'm a paedophile,' I imagined. Besides, Francesca Messina had already accused me of that when she had said I had stolen her daughter's childhood. How you can steal an eighteen-year-old's childhood was beyond me.

"It might come to that," said Liam. "In any case, they're coming in on Monday to talk to me. They say they've got evidence that you had feelings for Sofia whilst she was still a student at the school."

This confirmed my suspicions – yep – they obviously do think I'm a paedophile. "What sort of evidence?" I asked.

"Emails! Do you know anything about that?" Liam inquired.

I could see where this was going. They were going to try to use informal emails that I had sent to her as evidence that I was some sort of deviant individual. I am not a generally paranoid person, but the longer this conversation was going, the worse it was sounding. These people were really out to get me and they were going for me a few weeks after my mother had died when I was emotionally vulnerable, although I doubted that they knew about my mother.

"We exchanged emails, yes, but there was nothing bad in any of them. Some of them were over familiar perhaps, but that's all," I replied.

The meeting wound up and I went off to an examination invigilation. As I plodded round the hall, I realised that I no longer wanted to work in an environment where I felt unsafe. Liam had tried to bury the issue but I knew he would now be running scared of the Messinas. They wanted blood, and what's more, it was my fault - I had allowed this to happen by sending an insane message! I regretted that I hadn't followed my instincts and resigned in January. But I was so flattered that Liam and Robert wanted me to stay, that I had felt I owed them.

I set work for my afternoon classes, and went home sick. I could see how things were going to pan out, and it was grim. There was no point sticking around. It was time to go home, confess all to Lisa, and tell her that I would be resigning from my job. I was not unhappy to be leaving Farlbridge School, although I would have opted for a better way of ending my time there had I been given the choice. The only thing that really mattered to me now was my marriage.

"You're back early," said Lisa, as I came through the door at noon.

"I'm leaving Farlbridge," I replied.

It was the first anniversary of her father's funeral, and she was already feeling emotional that day. When I sat down and explained what had happened, she was upset, angry, feeling betrayed, and sad. She had some choice words for me, and I deserved every one of them. Yet, she also said, after we had both worn our hearts on our sleeves:

"I forgive you."

I was humbled by those three words. My atheist wife was showing me more Christian charity than her errant husband deserved, and she was certainly a greater example of Christian forgiveness than the Messinas who were practising Roman Catholics. It did not mean that Lisa was going to go easy on me, or stop feeling the hurt of my betrayal, but it did mean that we had a future together.

180

*****

I stayed off school for the next few days. There was no point my being there. On Monday afternoon, after Mrs Messina and Sofia had seen Liam Arnott, he telephoned me. He was not happy. He asked me about various things that they had said and the over familiar emails that I had sent. I pointed out to him that there was nothing in the emails that was particularly bad, and certainly nothing in the same league as my 'love' message.

He told me to come in for a chat with him at 7.45am the following morning. Lisa and I discussed what we thought would happen the next day. We both agreed that I would be back home by 9am!

When I went into school, Liam and Robert looked pretty grim-faced. I was asked once again about emails that were pretty innocuous. However, the Messinas were interpreting them in the most negative possible way, and Liam had a duty to investigate their complaint. Liam told me that Sofia had been particularly angry towards me and had really gone for me. It had got ugly.

At the meeting, what struck me most, was that Liam was not that concerned about me, but was more concerned by the Messinas and the possibility that they might sue the school. I thought he was worrying unnecessarily as in my mind, it was not the school they were angry with, but me. It had been six months since I had sent the message and I had apologised twice. I had not contacted Sofia at all during that time. Yet, according to Liam, she had come into school full of anger against me. To what extent this was her own anger, and to what extent she was reflecting the anger of her mother and father I did not know. All I knew was that this anger was real and it was directed not at the school but at me.

I told Liam and Robert the story of 'Secret Santagate' and how angry Mr Messina had been at the lad who had upset Sofia.

"So what do the Messinas want?" I asked Liam.

"Revenge!" He replied.

This told me all I needed to know. The priority from now on would be to assuage the anger of the Messina family, so that they didn't sue the school, and as part of this, I would have to go. This was panning out exactly as I had thought it would. What's more, I had had enough. They want my head on a platter, they can have it – it's only a fucking job.

"Apparently Sofia has a regular nightmare that you are chasing her across the school fields," added Mr Arnott.

It seemed to me that this revenge was more a farce. Am I to be held responsible for Sofia's nightmares now? I thought. Was her counselling only due to me? Could I really have traumatised her that much? How could one message have become such a drama six months on?

Liam officially suspended me and I was home shortly after 9am.

A few days later, Mr Arnott telephoned me, and seemed in a much more upbeat mood. He said:

"You know, we all make mistakes. We sent your emails to the LADO (Local Authority Designated Officer) and she said they were pushing boundaries but not criminal. There need not be a Police enquiry. What I hadn't told you was the allegation made against you by Sofia and her mother. They said that you had groomed her."

I was not at all surprised by this and I was not particularly impressed by Liam's relief, as he was just stating something that was plainly obvious to anyone with an ounce of common sense. It did not require a local authority lawyer to make that judgment. It had never occurred to me that I had done anything criminal – far from it – I had supported Sofia as best I could and had at worst been over familiar. I was deeply disappointed with the Messinas for making a false criminal allegation against me, but knew that their perspective was more emotional than rational. It occurred to me that perhaps Sofia had been much more emotionally involved with me than I had realised. May be she feels slighted by me, I thought. I hadn't contacted her for six months, and now she wants to remind me that she exists and can hurt me. Is it possible that her nightmare about my chasing her across the fields is an unconscious desire, as my counsellor suggested? I wasn't sure about any of this – all I knew was that I had poked the hornet's nest by sending my 'love' message and now was being stung as a result of my folly.

"What I'm looking for is a negotiated exit strategy," I said to Liam. I had already indicated that I was prepared to resign, so as far as I was concerned, it was just a question of negotiating terms. I had begun to move on from Farlbridge School in my mind.

Liam invited me to an investigation meeting on Wednesday 18th June. This meeting was in essence a negotiation. He had one more thing that he needed to secure from me, and that was my resignation. I was in a weak negotiating position so accepted his suggestion that I resign for 31st August. I sent him a letter resigning from that date. The following day he came back to me and told me that I would have to resign immediately, but that he would pay me holiday in lieu, which would financially equate to working until 31st August. So I resigned from 19th June. When we made this agreement, I said to Liam on the phone,

"I know you are a man of your word, so I am trusting you to honour this." Of course, I was wrong – he did not keep his word - I only got paid until 30th June.

Liam then came back to me saying that, despite my resignation, he would have to put me through another disciplinary as this was the procedure in 'safeguarding' cases. He was very apologetic for mucking me around and gave me the opportunity to withdraw my resignation. But, I was determined my resignation would stand, as I wanted out; and was convinced they would find spurious grounds on which to sack me otherwise. I was a bit puzzled as to why my case had been designated a safeguarding case, as I had not harmed a pupil in any way. My inappropriate message to Sofia had been sent after she had left the school. Liam said that if the disciplinary hearing found against me (which I knew it would), then my case would be referred to the Data and Barring Service (DBS) and the National College of

Teaching and Learning (NCTL). The NCTL is now known as the Teaching and Regulation Agency (TRA).

At this point, I was getting to a point of total despair. The DBS had the power to bar people from working with children and vulnerable adults, and the NCTL could stop you from working in any school in the country. I now realised that it was possible that Farlbridge might be the last school I ever taught in. And all because of one fucking stupid message. I sensed that the system was stacked against me. 'Surely things can't get any worse,' I thought to myself, 'surely this saga can't get any more farcical'.

Once again, I had got it wrong – things could and would get worse, nastier, and more ridiculous in ways that I had not anticipated.

CHAPTER 21

A WITCH HUNT BEGINS

"Claiming to be offended is a great way to elevate yourself at the expense of others: 'Look at me! I'm a much better person than you! And I judge you! I condemn you! Shame! Shame! SHAME!'"

Oliver Markus Malloy

Once a witch hunt has been started, it is easy for others to be sucked into it, especially when the system encourages the witch hunt. In my case, the witch hunt was started by the Messina family who had falsely got it into their heads that I was a paedophile who had groomed Sofia. I had allowed them to make this leap of imagination by my inappropriate message sent to her when she was an adult. I take the opinion that as far as Sofia's parents were concerned it was not in fact 'revenge' that motivated them in their determination to get me. With Sofia, I believed that something else was going on, but for her parents, there was a sincerely held belief that they needed to protect other young people from me. They had convinced themselves that what they were doing was the 'moral' thing to do. They are good people, but like all good people, they can get things wrong, just as I had. I felt sorry for the Messina family. According to Liam, Mrs Messina had told him that the incident had cost her her health, that the whole family was finding it difficult to cope and they were all seeing a psychiatrist. I still had a soft spot for Mrs Messina as she had reached out to me and it had been her telephone call that had been instrumental in my seeking counselling. Yet I could not help thinking that that the whole thing had been blown way out of proportion! How on earth could they all be in therapy because of a message that I had sent six months earlier?

On Monday 30th June 2014 a disciplinary meeting took place to consider further allegations against me. By this stage, I was so stressed by the witch hunt, that I felt there was no point turning up. I had already resigned and was in no doubt that the result of the disciplinary would not be positive for me. In hindsight, I should have attended, but at the time, Lisa and I were just fed up with the whole thing so we just went on holiday. Before the disciplinary meeting, I was sent a list of allegations made against me including one that said I had fallen below the required professional standards and another which accused me of not following the staff code of conduct. However, the allegation that particularly caught my eye, read as follows:

"That you were not open and honest about the full extent of your interactions with Sofia Messina when this was raised with you during the disciplinary investigation in February 2014."

The only problem with this allegation was that the premise of it was false. My interactions with Sofia were never raised with me during the disciplinary procedure except in two respects: I had been asked about messages I had sent on Facebook when Sofia had left the school and I had been asked about my feelings towards Sofia when she had been a student. Despite this, I had been open and honest throughout the whole process! I had told Liam during the investigation that Sofia used to greet me every morning in the house, that she used to 'pop up' on her own at odd times, that I had been fond of her, and that I had a good relationship with her and her mother. I had made it clear that I had worked closely with Sofia and had a humorous friendship with her and Lucy. Liam also knew that Sofia and her mother had held me in high regard.

I was angry that my honesty and openness had been impugned, and particularly angry with Liam because this allegation had come from him as investigating officer. I wondered if he were trying to imply that I had hoodwinked him in some way when I had not. Was he trying to justify his improperly constituted disciplinary hearing in February by claiming that I had been dishonest and misled him? Of course, I had lacked honesty and openness with my wife, but this was because the strategy had been devised to bury the bad news of my message, and I did not want to burden or hurt her with my emotional unfaithfulness.

The governor doing the disciplinary on the 30th June 2014, bizarrely, but predictably found this unfounded allegation of dishonesty substantiated despite any evidence that merited such a conclusion. She inappropriately questioned my 'honesty and integrity'. It would take me over a year to remedy this injustice.

*****

It was a relief when I was finally rid of Farlbridge School, however the real fight was still to come. I knew the school was going to refer my case to the NCTL and DBS as they now had to show that they had followed all proper procedures to the letter even though early on they had not. Liam Arnott did not think I was a safeguarding risk – he had told me as much, but in our current post-Saville paranoid era, when the mere mention of the word 'safeguarding' is mentioned, everyone panics and starts running for cover! Common sense goes out the window.

At this point I need to explain in a bit more detail what the roles of the National College of Teaching and Learning (NCTL) (now known as the Teaching Regulation Agency (TRA)) and the Data and Barring Service (DBS) are:

Both of these organisations are government agencies. The TRA is the regulatory body for teachers. Its main purpose is to hold teachers to account if they fall below acceptable professional standards. The TRA employs lawyers to act as 'prosecutors' in any case in which they decide that a teacher has fallen below acceptable standards. It also employs people to be 'panel members' that decide any individual case.

For each case there is a two-stage process. The first stage involves identifying whether the case merits a full hearing or not. The second stage is a public hearing involving three members of a TRA panel who decide whether a person is guilty of 'unacceptable professional conduct' (UPC). If one is found guilty of UPC, one can be either told off or prohibited from teaching in any school. Prohibition orders are indefinite, but can be reviewed after a minimum period of two years. In the most serious cases a review period is not granted and one is prohibited from teaching for life. The final decision on prohibition is not decided by the panel, but by a government appointed civil servant representing the Secretary of State for Education.

The DBS is a government organisation that can bar people from working with children and/or vulnerable adults. In order to decide whether one is barred from working with these groups, a 'harm test' is applied. Has that person done anything to significantly harm a child or vulnerable adult?

*****

In September 2014, I got letters from both the NCTL and the DBS telling me that I had been referred to them. This was of no surprise to me, but upsetting for Lisa. The NCTL made three allegations against me. These were that 1) I had engaged in an inappropriate relationship with Sofia, 2) I had been dishonest in my disciplinary meeting of 26th February 2014 and 3) I had not safeguarded pupils when consuming an inappropriate amount of alcohol whilst looking after pupils on a school trip to the Isle of Wight in 2010.

It was the third allegation that most amused me. I was not surprised that Liam had referred me for something that had happened four years earlier. I was in the witch hunt system now and the system wanted to know all about me! It is a curious facet of employment law that one can be tried repeatedly for the same offence, but in criminal law one can only be tried once (unless compelling new evidence is provided). I had already de facto been tried twice for my inappropriate message to Sofia, and now I would be scrutinised a third time! The infamous 2010 Isle of Wight trip also provided an opportunity to try to make me out to be a safeguarding risk!

I had a jolly good time on the Isle of Wight trip 2010, just as I had done on numerous school trips before! There were nine adults on the excursion. We were in charge of eighty-five Year 8 pupils. It was just over a month before I married Lisa, my mind was more directed at the preparations for this than anything else, and I was looking forward to the end of term. With me on the trip were a variety of colleagues including a couple of drinking partners. The trip passed off successfully, so I was surprised when I was hauled in to see the Headmaster six days after returning. Liam interrogated me about my drinking on the trip and I happily responded to his questions. Yes, I had drunk on both nights of the trip as had others. A few of us had arranged beforehand to take some wine on the trip and we had consumed most of it. No, I didn't drink in front of the pupils except when I had a beer whilst doing the barbecue. I pointed out that I had been the first person up the following day. I packed my tent early, and then went in to the canteen to do my turn in serving the pupils' breakfast.

It all seemed fairly petty to someone like me who had been on numerous school trips in which drinking alcoholic beverages was not only standard practice but virtually compulsory! However, the leader of the Isle of Wight trip in 2010 was twenty years younger than me and saw things differently. My problem was that I had form! On the Berlin,

Krakow and Prague trip that I led a month after Marie-Hélène died in 2008, I had drunk regularly as well (although never been drunk) and been fairly depressed. This had drawn the attention of one my colleagues, who claimed that the pupils were gossiping about it. When I came back, Robert Cook had hauled me in, and questioned me about it. I had pointed out that may be my colleague should have been a bit more understanding given that my wife had died a month earlier, especially as he had recognized how well organised and successful the trip had been.

Liam did a full investigation into our drinking habits during the 2010 Isle of Wight trip in which we all had to account for every bit of alcohol we had drunk. It was a bit over the top and I got the impression that Mr Arnott did not enjoy the exercise one bit. However, we all understood why he had to do it. At the end of it all, no further action was taken but Liam did send me a letter in which he asked me not to 'put us in a difficult position again.'

After the 2010 Isle of Wight trip, I came to the conclusion that the culture of drinking on school trips was now rather archaic, and we had entered a more sober and boring era in education. I was feeling a bit like a dinosaur in a neo-puritanical age. I resolved to do exactly as Liam Arnott had asked me and not drink on trips again. So, over the next four years at Farlbridge School, I refrained from drinking inappropriately on the six trips I attended.

Given that I had changed my habits, one could argue that Liam should not have referred me to the NCTL for my Isle of Wight hedonism in 2010. However, I had put in him in an even more difficult position with the Messina family so one could also argue that I was fair game for any accusation relating even remotely to 'safeguarding'. I was soon to find out that this was precisely the case. I thought we had finally got the measure of what we were dealing with. I was wrong – the accusations were about to get even more farcical and comedic.

CHAPTER 22

FARCE

"Even amidst tragedy there is laughter, sometimes farce. The degree of farce depends on who is running the tragedy."

Daniel Prokop, Leaving Netherland: Why little Boys Shouldn't Run Big Corporations

When the NCTL (known as the TRA now) got involved in my case, I decided it was time to get some legal support. I knew it was going to be expensive, but I found a lawyer who specialised in employment cases involving regulatory bodies. She was very good with an excellent knowledge of her legal specialism. Her name was Sophie. We were given two weeks to respond to the NCTL accusations.

Sophie knew exactly how to word things so that I appeared humble and contrite, however, at times I felt the wording was a bit too servile and groveling, so would insist on her toning it down. Once again, I had a problem, and my problem was that I did not want to grovel. I had already expressed remorse for my inappropriate message, and I was prepared to apologise again, but beyond that, I could not see that anything else that I had done warranted the attention it was getting. I was, however, prepared to play the game as I wanted to avoid the humiliation of a public hearing in which I would be named and shamed.

In our initial response, we admitted the first allegation that my relationship with Sofia had been inappropriate both before and after she left the school in that some of my emails to Sofia had been over familiar and of course I had gone bonkers after she had left. Seeing as we were dealing with a fascist regulatory body that insisted on ideological purity, I was prepared to go along with my lawyer's advice. However, some of the examples that the NCTL provided of inappropriateness were frankly risible, so my lawyer pointed out that 'Warm regards' or 'God bless' were not uncommon valedictions to emails. The NCTL got very excited by my 'such a sweetheart' comment that I had made after Sofia had put a coke in my office. I could not see why. If I had called Sofia 'my sweetheart', they might have had a point but calling someone 'a sweetheart' seemed somewhat mild to me, even if it wasn't my normal way of addressing students.

The second allegation of dishonesty I denied. I had not been dishonest so it was a no-brainer.

The third allegation about drinking more than was appropriate on the Isle of Wight was the most problematic one. I was guilty as charged and wanted to admit this one as I knew there was a load of evidence out there that had not yet been produced. My lawyer suggested we just deny it, and then see what was submitted. I went along with Sophie against my better judgement.

Another aspect of responding to the allegations was to provide evidence that I was a good teacher. This was not difficult as even the governor who questioned my honesty and integrity had written to me saying that 'there is no question that you have been a well-regarded member of the school community showing dedication to your students.' I thought it would be useful to get a reference from a member of the school community, so I contacted Daniel Bennett. He asked Liam if he could give me a reference, however Liam prevented him from doing so. Daniel texted me, saying, " Hi Charles, Bad news I am afraid. The Head would prefer me not to. I am sorry I can't help you but my hands are tied somewhat. Daniel." This was not the last time that Liam would try to obstruct Daniel.

After we had submitted our response, there were a few weeks when we heard nothing. Then, on 7th November 2014 I had further correspondence from the NCTL in which they produced further evidence of my 'inappropriate' drinking on the Isle of Wight and on my 2008 central Europe trip. But that was not the only thing they had added. They had decided to include a fourth allegation that left me stunned. I could not believe the pathetic depths of farce this witch hunt was descending into. The allegation read as follows:

4. Did not treat pupils with dignity and respect by:

i) Referring to Pupil Y as 'Marge Simpson' in or around 2009;

ii). Laughing at Pupil Z when she asked to study History at A Level in or around 2011.

Liam would no doubt argue that he had a legal obligation to hand over everything that was relevant to my case to the

NCTL, but that line of argument is complete nonsense. He was just scraping the barrel to fuck me over as best he could! The evidence for these allegations was based on a couple of brief exchanges of emails. In addition, I had not even been invited by Liam to talk face-to-face about these minor incidents, let alone been disciplined! However, looking back, I should not have been surprised that Liam sank to this level. He had already falsely accused me of dishonesty, so his commitment to the witch hunt was well established! Of course, by dragging up such ridiculous incidents, Liam showed himself to be a complete hypocrite. Earlier the same year, I had witnessed him humiliate one of my tutees to the point of making her cry. I was taken aback by his viciousness as I do not have it in me to talk to people in that way. The girl was a difficult pupil, but she did not deserve what she got from Liam Arnott that day!

What upset me most was that I had a really good relationship with my pupils and treated them and my colleagues with both respect and dignity, something that Liam and all my colleagues knew. The two incidents that were being dragged up were simply moments when I had let my professional persona down. When seen in context, they are not that bad, and reflect the sort of cock ups all teachers make.

In February 2009, there was an incident in which my Year 10 GCSE class was ribbing a girl (called Louise) about her alleged similarity to the cartoon character Homer Simpson. They said to me:

"Don't you think Louise looks like Homer Simpson?"

"No, not at all, she looks like Homer's wife, Marge," I replied.

It was a bit of a cheap joke and got me a hearty set of laughs. When you fancy yourself as a stand-up comedian in the classroom (and I did) there is always the danger that you forget you're not starring at the Hammersmith Apollo! The worst part of it was not that I had failed to show her dignity and respect, but that I had given the other pupils a 'gift' with which they could tease her. Louise seemed alright with my joke, and I checked to see that she was okay during the lesson. There was no indication she was upset so I forgot about it.

She went home that evening and was apparently devastated, crying in front of her father.

The next day, Louise's father, Mr Johnson, sent an email to Liam complaining I had done this. Then Mr Arnott forwarded the email to me, asking me what he was referring to. I promised to ring Mr Johnson and apologise straight away, which I did. I felt dreadful I had upset the poor girl, but she was perfectly pleasant when I found her the same day and apologised in person! Her father had a chat about it with me at the parent's evening the following day and that was the end of the matter.

Of course, this incident has a certain comedic value that was not lost on my colleagues when they found out about it! However, the TRA (NCTL) does not have a sense of humour – it is an organisation devoid of compassion, humour or perspective. When my lawyer was writing our response to this incident, she wanted me to repeat my apologies, and I refused initially. I resented being held to account for something that had been done and dusted six years previously, and proved nothing about me apart from the fact that I take risks with humour!

The allegation that I had laughed at a pupil who had wanted to take History A Level was also true. The girl did virtually no work in my lessons, so I had no idea she was interested in the subject. I was genuinely astonished, so laughed when she said she wanted to do it. Her mother, who was with her, took exception to my response as she thought her daughter was 'crestfallen' by it. It made for an awkward conversation and I subsequently apologised.

It was obvious that the NCTL and Liam Arnott were pathetically scrabbling round for anything that they could find to pin on me. In January 2015, I got an email from the bursar at Farlbridge School asking for my school laptop back which had been lying gathering dust at home. The school was so desperate to get their hands on the laptop that the bursar sent a member of staff with a minibus round to collect it from my house. It occurred to me that the school wanted to see whether they could find anything incriminating on it. Of course, I was totally relaxed about this as I knew that there was nothing to find!

*****

My lawyer responded to the 'Marge Simpson' and 'laughing' allegations admitting that, yes, on these two occasions I had not shown dignity or respect. I was not at all happy. The witch hunt was out to portray me as something I was not.

We waited to see whether my case would be referred to a full hearing or thrown out. Early in 2015, I heard that my case would indeed be referred to the NCTL for a full public hearing. The witch hunt had up to this point been remarkably successful, and I had no faith in the system, so I was not at all surprised by this outcome. I had by this point realised what a despicable organisation the NCTL was:

The TRA (NCTL) is a sort of modern day equivalent of the House Un-American Activities Committee (HUAC) which hunted down and expelled communists in 1950's America under the infamous Senator Joseph McCarthy.

A famous leaflet at the time declared "YOU can drive the reds out of television, radio and Hollywood." Just as the HUAC did, the TRA encourages allegations against teachers from any source and it encourages schools to dig up whatever they can to smear an individual. However, if you behave yourself and sign up to their agenda, you will be fine. It is a dualistic approach in which there are ideologically pure teachers who follow every regulation to the letter, and then there are the impure ones like me who believe in taking risks in our attempt to educate, who encourage students to think for themselves, challenge authority and urge students to be themselves rather than what other people want them to be.

The TRA expects teachers to conform to all the ideology they impose or they are cast out from the educational world. It is a simple worldview of good and evil, right and wrong, pure and impure. This dualistic approach of the TRA reminds me of the following quote from Arthur Miller's 'Crucible' which was written as a critique of McCarthyism:

"We conceive the Devil as a necessary part of a respectable view of cosmology. Ours is a divided empire in which certain ideas and emotions and actions are of God, and their opposites are of Lucifer. It is as impossible for most men to conceive of a morality without sin as of an earth without 'sky'. Since 1692 a great but superficial change has wiped out God's beard and the Devil's horns, but the world is still gripped between two diametrically opposed absolutes. The concept of unity, in which positive and negative are attributes of the same force, in which good and evil are relative, ever-changing, and always joined to the same phenomenon - such a concept is still reserved to the physical sciences and to the few who have grasped the history of ideas." Arthur Miller, The Crucible.

Of course, there are people who should be booted out of teaching, especially those who have abused children whether it be sexually, physically or psychologically. People with criminal convictions for possession of child pornography or those who bully and intimidate colleagues should be banned as well. But, the TRA regularly prohibits a whole raft of people who should not be banned, for misdemeanours that most fallible human beings make once in a while, publicly shaming them at the same time. Sometimes, it is not even the TRA panels that do the banning, but a government civil servant who was not at the hearing, who can overturn the decision of the three people best placed to make the decision. It would be equivalent in criminal law to the home secretary overturning the decision of a jury. Politicians get away with these natural injustices because these are civil proceedings. However, the High

Court can overturn decisions on appeal if one is prepared to risk £20K to £30K by going down that course of action.

There is an argument that politicians are just reflecting the state of society and may be society has become more intolerant and less compassionate. That is a depressing thought for those of us who espouse creative thinking, free speech, and want to educate the next generation to be genuinely independent minded. With free speech comes the possibility that one might offend others from time to time, but I would not be the first person to observe that in modern-day Britain we are developing a culture where people claim victimhood whenever anyone does even anything remotely offensive. The phrase 'snowflake' generation refers to exactly this – a generation that is easily offended and lacks the robustness to cope with the cut and thrust of debate.

I, personally, think it is wrong to label a whole generation as 'snowflakes' because in my experience there are plenty of young people who are good deal more robust than one might think. Yet our ability to 'offend' with views that are defensible, causes shock and horror.

So, coming back to my 'inappropriate message', what makes it so bad? Some would say that it was so bad because it was 'creepy' that a man so much older would express feelings for an eighteen-year-old. Yet, it is not uncommon for older men to have relationships with younger women and vice versa. Some would say it is bad because I knew Sofia from the age of thirteen, so it is a bit like a father falling in love with his daughter when she had reached the age of majority. But I was not her father – I was her teacher, and I did not groom her, and I did not abuse my position of trust with her. Just because one might have known someone as a child, that should not be a reason in itself, not to form a relationship with them as an adult. The TRA gets very worked up about this and regularly bans teachers who develop relationships with their students shortly after they have left a school. The assumption is that this teacher has been eyeing up all his pupils, looking for one they can prey on. There is an automatic assumption that their behaviour is predatory. However, that is often not the case. It is just they have met someone with whom they 'click' in a less than ideal situation, and then later form a romantic relationship with them. This was the case for me – I am not interested in teenage girls on a personal level – they are a bit like aliens to me. But after she had left the school, I had wrongly convinced myself that Sofia was different to any teenager I had ever met before.

Of course, my message to Sofia was inappropriate because a) I was married and b) I exhibited very poor judgement – such poor judgment that it constituted gross misconduct. I had got Sofia wrong. I should have realised that she did not have the emotional maturity to be able to deal with my expressing feelings towards her, and I should have realised that my love for my wife was a much more profound and meaningful thing than my obsession for Sofia. But I was in a bad place at that time and had lost the plot! But, perhaps worse than all this is the fact that I had broken a taboo. I had developed a fantasy, something that I suspect the vast majority of people do. Fantasies are normal and mine was a pretty standard one. However, to then act on or communicate that fantasy is the great taboo. Human beings are predictably judgmental and hypocritical; we condemn others for admitting to normal human failures that all of us have.

For me, getting it wrong, was an impetus to seek help so that I could be in a better place. I knew that I needed to deal with the guilt and trauma of my past. My mental breakdown had frightened me, so it was necessary to start on a path of psychological and spiritual healing. The first, and easiest part of this was to talk about Marie-Hélène, but the more difficult bit was to address the issue of Sofia. Counselling eventually helped me to put the pieces of the jigsaw together.

CHAPTER 23

THE PUZZLE SOLVED

"When I stand before thee at the day's end, thou shalt see my scars and know that I had my wounds and also my healing."

Rabindranath Tagore

When I started counselling with Sandra Sutton in early January 2014, I knew what the core problem was - it was guilt. Guilt about Marie-Hélène had eaten me up for years, and I needed to unburden myself, find peace, and move on. I also felt guilty about Sofia because I had hurt her emotionally and put her in a situation where she could no longer have either a real relationship with me or a virtual relationship through social media. And of course, I felt guilty that I had been emotionally unfaithful to Lisa.

Included in my guilt was something that happened in early 1997, about eighteen months before Marie-Hélène was diagnosed with brain cancer. We had only been married about six months. I woke up one day with a profound and unshakeable feeling that Marie-Hélène was going to die young.

How I came to have that premonition I still do not know. I wondered whether it was a psychic ability, or a message from God. However, looking back, I suspect it may have been that Marie-Hélène was already exhibiting the early symptoms of a serious illness, which I had picked up unconsciously. Whatever the source of my premonition about Marie-Hélène, the source of my guilt was that I then went on to tell Marie-Hélène about my premonition! I should not have done so, but I did. I said to her:

"I've got this awful feeling that you're going to die young M-H."

I was expecting her to say something like 'Don't be so stupid,' or 'You're going to die before me if you carry on talking like that.' Instead she just wept – she was extremely upset and the tears flowed liberally. I felt terrible, and then tried to row back on what I had said. However, it was too late – I had upset her profoundly. I have since wondered whether Marie-Hélène had experienced the same premonition.

*****

Sandra was a well-dressed lady twenty-years my senior. I liked her a lot as she oozed compassion that was not professionally affected, but entirely natural. She proved to be both a good listener and a good confidante. I told her in detail about Marie-Hélène's illness, her diagnosis, my problems with her family, how illness brought us closer together, and how remission tore us apart. I told her how I had split up with Marie-Hélène and then felt guilty that I wasn't with her when she needed me. I told her how I lost touch and hid my head in the sand. I told her how lonely and unsupported I felt. It all came out over months of counselling. Sandra was patient, compassionate, and listened to my story. She held my hand in a metaphorical sense and let me relive much of what I had experienced.

Counselling was difficult to begin with – I used to dread the sessions as they required me to bear my soul, and I worried that I would run out of things to say. But every time I had a session (once a fortnight), I found things that I needed to say, and after a while it became easier. I even started to enjoy it while it was happening but was nervous beforehand. I then worried that the counselling was self-indulgent and that it just encouraged my arrogance and narcissism. I discovered that I quite liked talking about myself with someone who was sympathetic. Yet normally I feel more comfortable in an environment where I am intellectually challenged, and people take the mickey out of me!

Just talking about my feelings and emotions in relation to Marie-Hélène made me feel better, but I did not make the leap to self-forgiveness until about four months in. We had just finished a session in which I had once again recounted my sense of failure and guilt, and talked about how isolated and lonely I had felt. Sandra said calmly at the end of the session:

"I would like you step outside yourself and imagine that you were the person listening to what you have just said. What would you say to that person who talked about their loneliness and isolation? What would you say to them about their guilt?"

I immediately felt a wave of compassion wash over me. I had been so self-absorbed and self-critical that I had failed to stand outside myself and seen things from a wider perspective. Yes, if someone had told me my own story, I would have told them that what happened was totally understandable and that they should not be so hard on themselves. I might even have said to them that they had endured too much, that they had gone beyond the call of duty; that it was incredible what they had put up with. I would not have told them that they were a victim or a hero, but I would have told them that they were human and had reacted in a normal human way to difficult circumstances, trying to balance their own needs with the needs of others. I would have told them to forgive themselves for any harsh words or misjudgements they had made. I would have told them that they were a fallible human and to accept that fact!

I am not totally cured of my guilt, but Sandra helped me to lighten the load, to make it manageable. I am now more able to carry my baggage without stumbling.

My counselling was also useful in helping me cope with the illness and death of my mother. Once again, Sandra was a good sounding board for what was happening. I was able to give her a running commentary on each aspect of my mother's illness – amputation, kidney failure, cancer diagnosis, mental decline and death. My relationship with Lisa had improved as well, so I had the support around me to work through the trauma of Christine's illness. Her peaceful death was for me a sacred moment - it had been a privilege to be there holding her hand.

*****

Even though my message to Sofia had been the impetus for my seeking counselling, I did not talk about her until the Messinas went all out to get me in June 2014. I had been in therapy for six months and it may seem surprising that Sofia had not been mentioned. However, I knew that my mid-life crisis had its roots in events that had preceded my relationship with Sofia, and addressing those events was much more important.

The other reason that I did not mention Sofia until six months into counselling, was that I felt shame about the message that I had sent and found it difficult to talk about. It was hard enough having to talk about it to my boss. I really did not want to mention it to anyone else if I could possibly help it. I still feel a little nauseous reading my inappropriate message, but seeing as it changed my life, I have come to embrace it, and own it, even though it reflects badly on me.

When I did talk to Sandra about my message and my relationship with Sofia, she was remarkably unperturbed and unsurprised by it all. I got the impression that she had heard a lot worse. I then regretted not talking about it earlier. As the focus of my counselling shifted away from Marie-Hélène to Sofia, I started to explore why I had become so emotionally involved with Sofia. I needed to understand what had been going on psychologically.

However, it was not just Sandra who helped me to join up all the dots. Lisa's input was equally as useful. The first 'lightbulb' moment came when I repeated to Lisa, Robert Cook's comment that my message had been 'self-destructive'. Lisa said:

"I'm no psychiatrist, but it's obvious to me that you have been punishing yourself for the guilt you feel about Marie-Hélène. That's why your behaviour has been so self-sabotaging."

This was a new idea to me, but it made a lot of sense. Yes, I had been punishing myself for past failures and guilt, and I had been doing this through different ways – by drinking too much alcohol; by a form of self-harming that involved picking my skin; by being withdrawn; by excessive levels of self-criticism; by playing over in my head traumatic events and memories; by irregular sleep patterns. And, finally, I had punished myself by sending an inappropriate message that was always going to harm me. I had been a 'snowflake' myself, exhibiting over-sensitivity to people and events, yet paradoxically being insensitive to others. I had become self-obsessed to an unhealthy degree. Of course, the thing that stopped me from naval gazing was teaching. It took me out of myself and allowed me to help and serve others. But, I had punished myself by destroying that too.

It made me wonder if I had been suffering from a form of Posttraumatic Stress Disorder (PTSD). When I suggested this to Sandra, she was non-committal, perhaps because this was not her psychological speciality. To a certain extent, I'm not sure how much these labels help or mean much, but I wanted to understand as much as I could about what had been going on psychologically. Of course, I cannot compare what I have experienced to people who have gone through the horrors of war and been diagnosed with a more obvious form of PTSD. However, I wondered whether a constant stream of witnessing illness and death of loved ones between 1993 and 2008, had left me with a level of trauma that most people did not go through in their twenties and thirties. It would explain why I had finally cracked after my father-in-law died in 2013.

Lisa also helped me understand why I had got involved with Sofia. When she found out about my emotional infidelity, she was obviously angry and upset. It still hurts. However, she also wanted to understand why I had got involved with this particular girl. Lisa said to me:

"Do you have a photo of her?"

"Not on her own, but I think I might have one of her when she was in my form."

"Show it to me."

I found the photo, which contained a group of 20 students, boys and girls, and presented it to Lisa on the computer screen.

Lisa pointed straight at Sofia and said, "That's her, that's Marie-Hélène!"

"How on earth did you know who Sofia was from a group photo?" I replied, not quite understanding what she meant.

"Because she's the split of your dead wife! Can't you see it?"

I could not. It may be surprising that I had never noticed a physical similarity between Sofia and Marie-Hélène, but I don't remember Marie-Hélène's face that well. I remember that she was beautiful, but could not tell you why, I remember her personality, her presence, and I remember her emotions. However, I've never been one for analysing faces that much. I'm not the 'super-recogniser' Lisa is. I was sceptical about Lisa's thesis that Sofia looked like Marie-Hélène, because Lisa had never met Marie-Hélène. She had only seen her in photos.

Later on, after Lisa had stunned me with this new angle on Sofia, I got a photo of a young Marie-Hélène, before she became ill, and put it alongside the photo of Sofia. 'Fuck me,' I thought, 'Lisa's right – there is a remarkable resemblance!'

And then I thought about all the unconscious connections I might have made between Marie-Hélène and Sofia. How I had used 'God bless' in an email to Sofia when I had said it to Marie-Hélène the first day we met. How excessively concerned I had been with Sofia's health condition in the same way as Marie-Hélène's health had become a preoccupation, and how I had cried after 'Secret-Santagate' because I had unconsciously made a connection between Sofia's suffering and Marie-Hélène's suffering! Sofia had only been fifteen at the time! It occurred to me that this unconscious transferential relationship might even have started when I first met her at the age of thirteen, even though consciously she had made very little impression on me. It was only six weeks after Marie-Hélène died that I met Sofia, so may be in my vulnerable state, I had started the unconscious transference then! It was a pretty scary thought, but I remember thinking when I first met Sofia – 'there's something different about this girl – what is it?'. Perhaps, it wasn't that she was different, but that she was remarkably similar in looks and personality to my dead wife. Could I have been transferring unconscious feelings on to one so young?

I then started analysing similarities in personality between Sofia and Marie-Hélène. They were both hard working, determined and focused. They both lacked self-confidence but were resilient. They were both awkward and had few friends. They both came from close-knit families with mothers who were religiously conservative.

Then I thought about how angry and nasty towards me Sofia had been when she came into school and accused me of grooming her – it showed passion, and it showed that she cared. Sofia was passionate, tenacious and extreme, which are very attractive qualities to me. She was very much like the young Marie-Hélène who was also passionate and caring, drove too fast and was go-get-it! Sofia told me when she was learning to drive that she drove too fast and her instructor had to tell her to slow down! And, like Marie-Hélène, Sofia is basically a sweetheart – a kind, oversensitive, loving young woman. The difference is that Sofia has a ruthless streak that my first wife did not have. And, boy, did I find out how ruthless Sofia could be!

It also occurred to me I might even have had unconscious romantic feelings towards her in her last year at Farlbridge School. Those romantic feelings exploded into a conscious falling in love because I was unconsciously going through the pain and loss of losing Marie-Hélène again (in the form of Sofia) and was desperately trying to hold on to her. There was no professional duty of care inhibiting those feelings once Sofia had left Farlbridge. Yet I knew consciously that I could never have a real relationship with Sofia, so tried unsuccessfully to distance myself from her.

By December 2013, I had become an emotional and psychological wreck. I was still punishing myself for the guilt I felt about Marie-Hélène. Add to that, the self-loathing I felt for having feelings towards Sofia, and my self-punishing tendencies had reached a critical level. I had lost all sense of perspective. I sent a message that was selfish, self-sabotaging and self-obsessed.

"It was complex grief," stated Sandra. "Your complex grief had been the catalyst for the transferential relationship you had developed towards Sofia."

"So what was I trying to do?"

"Reparation?" suggested Sandra.

"I think it might have been worse than that – I think it might have been 'resurrection'. I suspect I might have been trying to bring back Marie-Hélène in the form of Sofia. I was trying to bring back the young Marie-Hélène full of energy and hope for the future, trying to relive the good times."

"Yes, reclaiming your youth with a younger woman. I think it may have been a mid-life crisis as well," speculated Sandra.

"Do you think my mid-life crisis was worse because of everything I had been through – all the trauma and my complex grief?"

"That's more than possible," replied Sandra

Then, I started to get it. Poor Sofia had been the victim of my complex grief without realising it. No wonder she had been so angry and confused. And Lisa had been a victim of it as well. My unresolved grief and guilt had wreaked havoc on those I cared about because I was punishing myself for past failures.

"So what if I teach again and meet another girl who reminds me of Marie-Hélène. Isn't there a danger that I might just repeat the same mistake again?" I asked Sandra.

"I have seen you grow and develop throughout this process," said Sandra, "you are in a much better place, and you now understand how your complex grief affected you, and how your guilt led you to be self-destructive. Now that you understand what was going on, I don't think that you would repeat the same behaviour."

So it was, that when I went to my hearing at the NCTL in the summer of 2015, the panel had this explanation of my complex grief and the unconscious transferential relationship I had developed with Sofia before them. They had Sandra's professional opinion that I would not repeat the same behaviours. Sandra had written it all down in a letter. They were completely unmoved. "The panel does not accept that this provides an adequate explanation or excuse for Mr King's conduct," they wrote.

CHAPTER 24

THE HEARING

"There is no greater tyranny than that which is perpetrated under the shield of the law and in the name of justice."

Montesquieu, The Spirit of the Laws

In February 2015 I got a letter from the Data and Barring Service (DBS) telling me that it would not be appropriate to bar me from working with children and vulnerable adults. They had applied a harm test and come to the conclusion I had not harmed a child in my care nor a vulnerable adult. They had taken into account that my inappropriate message to Sofia had been sent after she had left the school. I knew I was no risk to children. I had not been a risk to Sofia, nor did I represent a risk to any other child. The DBS could see that.

However, I still had to face the NCTL which was going to put me through a hearing that would publicly shame me whatever the outcome of the panel hearing. Now bearing in mind that the only seriously unacceptable thing I had done happened seven months after I had last taught Sofia, I could not for the life of me understand what public interest there was in humiliating me like this. I had done nothing even remotely criminal and nothing that had harmed a child. No, this was clearly a witch hunt sanctioned by the Department for Education. It was cruel, mean and unjust. In arguing for this state sponsored McCarthyism, one could say that public humiliation provides a deterrence to others. Prohibit a few of the good ones, show them up to be the dangerous free-thinking liberals that they are, and everyone else will fall into line. To be fair, if I had been thinking about how fascist and cruel the NCTL was, I would never have sent my inappropriate message!

Of course, that is how executive power often works. However, it is a depressing thought that teachers now work in an environment where they are constantly watching their backs, where every complaint or mistake may come back to haunt them years later when the TRA (NCTL) decides to launch a witch hunt against them. The government wonders why it has a recruitment crisis. I'm sure one of the reasons is the insecurity and paranoia that now exists in the profession, created by the government itself. And, incidentally, my critique of the TRA is not a party-political criticism. I have been a member of the Conservative Party, have liberal social values, and believe in welfare capitalism. However, when a government gets things wrong, it is important to exercise one's free speech and highlight it.

In March 2015, Lisa and I found a beautiful large, four-bedroomed house in the North Cotswolds with a fabulous rural view over hills. It was idyllic and provided the perfect place to move to with her mother, who could no longer look after herself. I had long hankered after a bucolic existence, and we had both had enough of the metropolis.

Shortly after we moved to the Cotswolds, my NCTL hearing took place. My lawyer Sophie had recommended a barrister to me who had plenty of experience in cases relating to regulatory bodies. Her name was Julie Davidson. Julie was a tall, blonde woman, imposing both in height and intellect. I imagined that she must have been Captain of the school netball team when younger, but never asked her whether that had been the case. She was very well spoken, confident, and compassionate. She had seen it all, knew the NCTL game, and was adept at playing it.

Of course, I was up against it as I had no illusions about how ruthless the TRA could be. The only good thing about the TRA (NCTL) is that it employs panellists from various backgrounds to hear cases, who act as judges in the case. I imagine that some of the panellists are compassionate people with empathy who understand the pressures of teaching. Certainly, TRA panels often surprise people with their free thinking and independence. They sometimes do not impose prohibition orders when perhaps they should do. However, the secretary of state's representative is always on hand to correct their independent stance. I read of one case where the panel did not impose a prohibition order on a teacher who had received a caution for possession of a video that contained a naked image of someone under eighteen. I do not know all the details of the case, but the secretary of state's decision maker overturned their decision and banned the teacher for life! Of course, when it comes to panels, it is a bit of a lottery. Either you get a panel that is fair-minded and independent, or you get a panel that lets their prejudices obscure the truth. Some teachers are lucky, some are not.

*****

When I got to the NCTL hearing, Julie warned me that it was a very serious, stuffy affair in which it was necessary to mind ones p's and q's. What I had not realised, was how brutal it was going to be. In my naivety, I imagined that I would be attending a hearing in which evidence would be presented dispassionately, witnesses would give their account, my barrister would respond to the evidence, the panel would ask a few questions, and then they would come to a decision. This had been my experience of previous disciplinary procedures when I had carried them out as a senior manager and governor of a state school.

It was not at all like that. It was set up like a criminal court with a prosecutor (known as the 'presenting officer') in the form of a lawyer, hired by the NCTL to besmirch my name in anyway he could, and counsel (my barrister) to defend me. I had not expected to be treated like a criminal, but that is exactly what happened. Within five minutes of the presenting officer's introduction, I was horrified. He was describing someone who I did not recognise – a teacher who represented a risk to children, who did not care about their welfare, who was a chancer, and showed them little respect and dignity. I could not believe it - I had spent twenty-seven years working to educate two generations of young people, developing good relationships with both my pupils and colleagues. I was an excellent tutor with a reputation for being both caring and conscientious. I had never harmed a child or abused my position of trust, and this young lawyer was treating me with a disdain that beggared belief. I was huffing and puffing, shaking my head and rolling my eyes. Julie had to call a recess so that she could calm me down and tell me I wasn't helping myself. It was state-sanctioned slander and I could not do anything about it. And all because I had sent a fucking stupid message that had offended a young adult.

At this point, I should point out that I did not feel anything personal against this young lawyer. He was doing the hatchet job that the NCTL was paying him to do. Bizarrely, he had a surname that was the same as my mother's maiden name. 'Perhaps we're related,' I thought to myself, 'now that would be an irony'! Over the three days of my hearing I grew to respect him for the job that he was doing. My barrister was so impressed by him that she tried to offer him a pupillage!

The panel was inevitably three white middle-class, middle-aged individuals. There was a chairwoman who had a passing resemblance to Anne Hegerty from 'The Chase' but lacked her charm, an older woman with grey hair who was perfectly pleasant but a little dim, and a tall, intense teacher representative who seemed both fascinated and contemptuous of me in equal measure. It did not take me long to realise that they were all devoid of empathy and emotional intelligence so I came to the conclusion within the first ten minutes that I was fucked. Basically, they were simply not my sort of people – I did not feel an affinity with any of them, even though I tried hard to pierce through the armour of their officialdom. And to be fair, I don't think I was their cup of tea either! They were assisted by a legal advisor who was a tall, stern looking character equally stuck up his own arse.

It is important to set out what I was being accused of, and when one reads it in black and white, one can see how pathetic the whole thing was. I have already talked about the Isle of Wight jolly, the Marge Simpson farce, and laughing at a lazy pupil, which were allegations 3 & 4, but the 'serious' stuff (if you can call it that) was contained in allegations 1 & 2:

1. Pursued an inappropriate relationship with Pupil X (Sofia) by

    i) sending her a message saying, "I just can't stop loving you [Pupil X]";
    ii) exchanging private messages with her via Facebook;
    iii) sending one or more emails:
        to Pupil X's personal email account and to Pupil X from his own personal email account;
    iv) addressing her as "sweetheart" in an email;
    v) sending her an online birthday card;
    vi) engaging in one to one conversations with her in his classroom.

2. Was dishonest by not revealing his behaviour as in allegation 1, during the disciplinary meeting held on 26th February 2014.

When one knows that allegations 1.i) and 1.ii) happened after Sofia had left the school (so was no longer 'Pupil X', but 'Adult X'), it does raise these questions: 'What the fuck?

221

Is that all you've got?' But of course, having dug up the huge scandals of 'Drinking-gate', 'Marge-gate' and 'Laughing-gate', this teacher was banged to rights! The witch hunt was bound to succeed!

Apart from me, there was only one other witness called at the hearing and that was Liam Arnott. Both the NCTL and my legal team had agreed that we would not call Sofia to be a witness. I don't even know whether she knew in advance about the hearing though I suspect she did. I think it would have been difficult for her, and I was glad that the NCTL had the humanity to spare her having to turn up and be a witness in front of me. At least, in this respect, common sense prevailed. Neither were the former students involved in 'Marge-gate' and 'Laughing-gate' called.

We had admitted allegations 1, 3 & 4 (as ridiculous as it all was) and I accepted that my inappropriate message was 'unacceptable professional conduct.' It was painful having to co-operate with the NCTL witch hunt, and I would not do it again. It involved a load of bullshit legal speak and a certain amount of written grovelling that I felt uncomfortable with. However, I was prepared to go along with the advice of my lawyers if that meant clearing my name. However, there was no way I was going to accept allegation 2. I had not been dishonest and was determined to show this.

Of course, the NCTL was bent on painting me out as a liar and a criminal in whatever way they could. Their presenting officer came up with a fantastical thesis that I was a financially poor teacher desperate to hold on to my job, and that I lied about my relationship with Sofia in order to hold on to my only means of supporting myself and my wife who had given up work. His theory that I was poor was rather undermined by the fact that I had employed a legal team at significant expense to represent me! When Liam had first asked me about my message, he had asked me whether I had done anything criminal. I had replied that I had done nothing illegal. The NCTL lawyer tried to frame this as me trying to justify my message by arrogantly saying 'I've done nothing illegal'! It was a complete inversion of the truth. He tried to imply that after I had sent the message, I had been worried that I had done something criminal. This annoyed me, and he knew he was sailing close to the wind by trying to infer criminal guilt or intent and I was surprised that the Chair of the panel allowed him to go as far as he did, when she had already interrupted my lawyer on several occasions. Eventually, I just said to him:

"Nothing I have done even remotely satisfies any test of criminality."

That shut him up as far as this line of questioning was concerned.

However, the dishonesty allegation first came from Liam Arnott, so ultimately, it came down to a battle between him and me. I doubted that I would win the war, but I was determined to win this battle. I had been a complete idiot and plonker in sending my inappropriate message, but I was not a liar, and resented being labelled as one.

When Liam gave his testimony as a witness, he chose, like me, to swear an oath on the Bible saying that he would 'tell the truth and nothing but the truth.' Liam looked distinctly awkward and uncomfortable in the hearing. My feelings towards him were ambivalent – on the one hand, I felt sorry for him as I knew this was a very difficult situation for him. On the other hand, I felt like punching his lights out for being such a git.

He confirmed when questioned by my barrister that he had kept the investigation into my inappropriate message within 'tight parameters.' He denied that he had told me in advance of the February disciplinary meeting that I would not be sacked, saying, "It would be a strange sort of disciplinary meeting if all options were not available," yet that's exactly what it was – a very strange meeting where the outcome was predetermined! As the disciplinary panel wrote - they were 'surprised to note that he intended to conduct the hearing despite the fact that he had carried out the investigation.'

The problem for Liam in trying to prove that I had lied in the meeting of 26th February, was that his own minutes of the meeting showed that I had not! The panel stated the following in their findings:

'The panel observes that, in answer to a question from the presenting officer, Witness A (Liam) said that at the disciplinary meeting on 26th February 2014, "I asked directly whether there was anything else I needed to be aware of". However, in answer to questions from Ms Davidson (Julie), Witness A confirms that the minutes of the disciplinary meeting on 26th February 2014 is an accurate record of what was said. In the minutes of the meeting, there is no reference of such a direct question being asked of Mr King."

The panel also stated:

'[Witness A (Liam)] also hoped that, as written in the minutes of the disciplinary meeting of 26th February 2014, the matter "will remain private" and contained, bearing in mind also that Pupil X's (Sofia's) mother had been at pains to insist that Pupil X and her father should not be aware of the fact that Pupil X's mother had brought this to the attention of the school.'

It was a relief when the panel found the allegation of dishonesty not proved, and it was good that Liam admitted that he was trying to contain what had happened. Of course, he had lied when in his written submission he had claimed he asked me whether there was anything else he needed to be aware of, and he denied that he had said 'Don't' when I suggested I tell my wife. He did, however, admit that I had done 'an excellent job' at Farlbridge School, not that the panel was interested in my talents as a teacher.

The panel had at the very least exposed the truth in respect of the lying allegation. I was disappointed that a governor at Farlbridge School had inappropriately questioned my honesty and integrity because of this allegation. And why Liam pursued this false allegation of lying against me, I doubt I will ever know. It is up to him to answer that question, but my own theory is that he was just trying to cover his own arse and felt a duty to try to bury me as deep as possible in order to avoid the school being sued by the Messinas.

Liam admitted that he had said that the Messina family wanted 'revenge' at the hearing, and when asked by my barrister whether he had been concerned that they would sue the school, he stated "Yes, and they still might." Of course, the only basis they would have had for suing the school would be if it had not followed proper procedure. And proper procedure had not been followed when Liam investigated my case and then set himself up as the sole judge of it!

Another aspect of Liam's testimony also exposed a lie. Before the final hearing, Daniel Bennett had been approached a second time to give me a reference. Once again, Daniel approached Liam about this and Mr Arnott tried to prevent him from doing so. At the hearing Liam explained that by giving a reference, Daniel would have been in a conflict of interests. I could see Liam's point of view – the school was involved in a process that involved hunting down a witch, so it would be curious if it then helped the witch! Of course, this argument sounds reasonable but is totally outrageous – there is no conflict of interest in exposing the truth and giving an accurate reference for someone. Arnott was simply trying to obstruct justice! Liam, however, went further than he needed and said that Daniel agreed that it would be a conflict of interests. What Liam did not realise, was that Daniel did give me a reference which we presented to the panel. The reference clearly shows Daniel did not think it was a conflict of interests to help me, but rather had been obstructed by Liam! His email read as follows:

"Dear Ms Jones (assistant to Sophie)

I am sorry but I am unable to write a reference for Charles. He worked for me as a reliable tutor for Year 9, 10 and 11. He was very organised and the children liked him and I always thought he had their best interests at heart. He was very good at communicating what he was doing and would keep me up to date with any developments in the tutor group. He was also a very sociable colleague, who frequented the staffroom regularly. He was well liked by staff.

I hope this helps.

Kind regards,

Daniel Bennett"

As far as I am concerned, there are only two people who comes out as heroes in my story. They are my wife, Lisa, and Daniel Bennett.

*****

I had admitted unacceptable professional conduct in respect of my inappropriate message, so whether or not I was going to be banned, came down to the discretion of the panel. The panel took the most negative possible stance on me that they could. It was shocking. The worst thing they wrote was this:

"There is strong public interest consideration in respect of the protection of pupils given the serious findings of an inappropriate relationship with Pupil X (Sofia)"

They could not have been either nastier or more wrong. The witch hunt had officially declared me to be a witch – a danger to children! How dare they! How dare they say that children needed to be protected from me! It makes my blood boil! Who the fuck are these people? There was no evidence that I had hurt or harmed a pupil or was a danger to children. It hurts to be labelled in this way and it always will, but then in the seventeenth century I would have been put on a stake and burned, which would have hurt even more!

Of course, the panel was not interested in me. When my barrister was asking me about my background, the Chairwoman of the panel interrupted her and said,

"We know all this - can we move things on?"

I was livid although it would not have helped my case to have shown it. I sat there thinking, 'You don't care about my story, my narrative and the pain that I have carried over years – you have no ability to empathise with me.' At a couple of points in the proceedings I felt so crushed by the whole thing that I wanted to cry, but was not prepared to show that I was humiliated to that extent. However, I did show remorse for upsetting Sofia, and even the panel acknowledged that.

The panel had all the mitigation in front of them but it did not make the slightest difference. The teacher panellist seemed particularly offended and alarmed that I did not know what the government's framework on safeguarding was. I also said that I doubted whether many teachers did. For me, safeguarding was about common sense, and no, I did not spend hours as a teacher reading government publications, and I suspect very few teachers do. However, once again, my honesty counted against me!

One thing that the panel wrote that was correct was this:

"When giving evidence, and although he showed remorse, he did not give the panel the impression that he truly recognised the seriousness of the combined nature of his conduct."

They were right! It was difficult to take seriously a witch hunt that had been started because I had wrongly been accused of being a paedophile! It was difficult to take seriously having to explain relatively minor incidents that had happened years earlier, for which I had apologised and moved on. I could not understand why I was being bashed over the head for things that were so historical.

In the end, the panel handed me down an indefinite prohibition order that could be reviewed after the mininum period of two years. They were at pains to emphasise what a serious case mine was (which of course it was not) yet despite declaring that 'this is a very serious case' as if they were trying to convince themselves that the witch hunt was justified, they still recognized that no more than a minimum review period was warranted!

The panel made wrong assumptions about me because they were caught up in a McCarthyite system and were blind to its cruelties. We rightly criticise people for 'trolling' – for publicly humiliating and insulting people on social media. However, by publicly shaming a good person who had been widowed and traumatised, and experienced a mental breakdown, the NCTL descended to the same level as trolls. This for me, is the worse aspect of what the TRA does, using 'public interest' as an excuse to publicly humiliate good people and destroy their reputations – people who have done nothing criminal, and have not done anything to harm a child. The TRA, as presently structured, will continue with its witch hunts in this way, which makes teaching a highly precarious job to undertake.

About two weeks after the panel came to their decision, their report was published on the NCTL website. Every journalist knows that the NCTL is a well of information about the peccadillos of teachers, and on slow news days these receive more attention than they deserve! This is what happened in my case.

CHAPTER 25

AFTERMATH

"If you don't read the newspaper, you're uninformed. If you read the newspaper, you're mis-informed."

Mark Twain

I always anticipated that the NCTL report on me would get coverage in the Press and that is exactly what happened. The reason I expected my case to be noticed, was that it contained a gift to journalists. That gift was 'Marge Simpson'! Marge-gate was genuinely funny. Sophie told me that she and Julie almost wept with laughter over it. "We thought it was a very witty comment," Sophie told me. Obviously, there is a serious side that a girl was upset by it, however, bearing in mind that my 'Marge' comment was made back in February 2009, I'm hoping the girl (who would currently be twenty-four) would now see the funny side of it herself.

Of course, the press did pick up on other elements of my story, sometimes comically. The Daily Express ran with the headline:

"History teacher banned for inappropriate relationship." The article started with the paragraph: "A HEAD of History sent inappropriate messages to an ex-pupil, got drunk on a school trip and called another child "Marge Simpson."

I was amused by the use of the 'HEAD' in capital letters, emphasizing my seniority. However, I laughed out loud when I saw the picture if Homer and Marge Simpson that they had included in the article. Lisa cried as she hated me being humiliated and felt vicariously humiliated herself. I was fairly relaxed and amused about the whole thing as I was expecting it and warned Lisa that it would happen.

The Times Educational Supplement had the headline: "Teacher who likened pupil to Marge Simpson is struck off," and a local paper went with, "Disgraced Farlbridge School History teacher banned for rude messages and likening pupil to Marge Simpson."

The word 'disgraced' summed it up well. The NCTL had disgraced me and declared that children needed to be protected from me! However, I did not feel a disgrace – I felt I had been a successful and caring teacher who had contributed a significant amount to society.

I have no complaints about the Press coverage of my hearing. A free press is essential to democracy. The newspapers quoted accurately from the NCTL report, which was of course damning. The papers reported things out of context but that is quite normal. More worryingly, the NCTL panel also failed to appreciate the contexts of things that had happened despite these contexts being explained to them! I cannot blame newspapers for the NCTL's lack of insight or compassion. The truth is of course, there was no justification for making any of the allegations against me public, as all of them were relatively minor compared to what some teachers get up to! But by doing so, the NCTL gave the press titbits. Journalists love morsels as well as main meals. As Eric Cantona said in a 1995 press conference after famously 'kung-fu' kicking an abusive football spectator:

"When the seagulls follow the trawler, it's because they think sardines will be thrown into the sea."

*****

Liam Arnott made a pathetic attempt at damage limitation when my case became public. Once again, he lied by saying to parents and teachers that the school had followed proper procedure when it became aware of the allegation in January 2014, when even the NCTL report had pointed out that he should not have judged a case he investigated! He said how 'sad' the situation was, which was just a way of deflecting from his own dishonesty and trying to appear decent. Of course, the truth is that his conduct had been totally duplicitous. He was determined to bury me, and did so whilst putting on his usual false front of reasonableness and mild-mannered-ness. Fortunately, the NCTL panel's cynicism was not just directed towards me, but towards Liam as well.

I had already moved to the Cotswolds when my panel hearing took place. So when my situation became public, I felt happily remote from Farlbridge School. I am in a fortunate position in that I do not need to work, however I do work, for felt it was important to get myself back out there and make a contribution to society – to serve in a useful way. So, shortly after my NCTL hearing, I got my dream job – delivering groceries for a well-known supermarket! I get paid for driving round the Cotswolds and I meet a lot of interesting people from diverse backgrounds. It is not an intellectually challenging job but it is, like teaching, rewarding at a human level.

And I could, if I chose, work with children (but not in a school), because although one government agency (the NCTL) declared there was a public interest in protecting children from me, another government agency (the DBS) declared that it would not be appropriate to prevent me from working with children. I am banned, but not barred! This is what you might call 'schizophrenic government' and does rather back up my argument that the TRA (NCTL) is simply a McCarthyite which hunting organ of the Department for Education.

So what can we conclude from my story apart from the fact that 'shit happens!'? I hope that we can learn from it that tragedy shapes, forms and influences us as we travel through life, that we all make mistakes, and that we all fall short of the ideal of what we should be.

However, I have learnt that guilt and self-punishment serves little purpose. I have also found out how narrow-minded and judgmental humans and human institutions can be. Of course, I did a cross a line with my inappropriate message, but by crossing that line, I discovered a huge amount. I discovered a lot about myself and I found out who my real friends were. I found out that I was loved more than I could have possibly imagined. I discovered that life is often a comedy and a farce, and yes, sometimes it is so bizarre, that you just 'could not make it up!' I was banned from teaching unjustly, but ultimately that is neither here nor there. It is but a small reflection of a society that has lost its ability to be at ease with itself, that looks for demons where there is none, that obsesses over small things and loses sight of the bigger picture.

The bigger picture is this: 'Love your neighbour as yourself' and 'Forgive those who tresspass against us.' It is in relationships that we find true fulfilment. I have been sad and depressed and selfish, and failed in relationships that were unhealthy. However, I have found redemption and healing in positive, life affirming friendships, a marriage and family. We fail every day but also succeed. We are human beings who stumble sometimes, and shine at other times. Most people are good and kind, but too many let themselves get dragged down by their own prejudices and insecurities. They let themselves become blind to compassion and truth and are too quick to judge other harshly. Rise up, and be free, fly like a bird, let your creativity, independence and love soar above the clouds of intolerance. Be yourself, for yourself, and for all those you serve.

AUTHOR'S NOTE

'An Inappropriate Message' is a true story, true in the sense that I took care to recount the events as accurately as I could recall them. Being a first-hand account, it is necessarily subjective in nature, and others may interpret things that have been said or done differently.

My motivation for writing my story was to tell the truth about events that could happen to anyone in the twenty-first century. These are times where everyone is subject to a level of scrutiny and potential humiliation that is unprecedented in human history. We live in a world in which one non-criminal misdemeanour can destroy someone if an offended person jumps up and down enough and makes a fuss. It is a world where a sense of perspective has been lost. As you have read in the story, it does not take much to destroy someone's career and reputation. With this is mind, I tried to carefully balance telling the truth, with a wish to protect other people's anonymity. I have therefore changed the names of certain central characters, places and details. I am particularly keen to protect the anonymity of the Messina family at the centre of this story. I like to think that they are good people and anything they did to hurt me was on the basis of a misunderstanding as to the type of person I was, in a situation where I was not able to communicate with them. I bear no malice towards Sofia or her parents.

I hope you enjoyed reading my story, which is a cautionary tale for anyone considering taking up teaching in the UK in the twenty-first century. My intention is not to discourage people from entering what was for me a hugely rewarding profession. However, if my story can help us move away from the current McCarthyite tendency to dictate a rigid set of standards and beliefs, and then hunt down and condemn those who fall below them in any way, then hopefully I will have done some good by writing it. We should be living in a more tolerant society and it saddens me that compassion is not a more valued quality in public life, even if it exists in abundance at the level of friendships and family relations.

We all have tragedies and traumas in our lives and these affect us in different ways. If my story can also help others to understand how these past events shape us and leave us vulnerable to episodes of mental fragility, I shall also have done a worthwhile thing by writing it.

I would also like to thank all those who gave me invaluable feedback on my story, and helped me in editing and structuring this book.

Finally, I hope that my story does not deter people from expressing themselves freely and openly, as I am keen to promote the liberal values that seem sometimes to have been lost in our neo-puritanical and politically correct society.

I raise a glass to you all!

Charles King

Printed in Great Britain
by Amazon